A History of Longridge
and
its People

by
Joseph M. Till

Carnegie Publishing, 1993

A History of Longridge

and

its People

by

Joseph M. Till

Carnegie Publishing, 1993

To RAE

A History of Longridge and its People
by Joseph M. Till

First published, April 1993

Text copyright, © Joseph M. Till, 1993

Published by Carnegie Publishing Ltd., 18 Maynard Street, Preston PR2 2AL
Designed and typeset in 10/12 Times by Carnegie Publishing Ltd.
Printed and bound in the UK by the Alden Press, Oxford

British Library Cataloguing-in-Publication Data
Till, Joseph M.
    A History of Longridge and its People
    I. Title
    942.7685
    ISBN 0–948789–86–7 (casebound)
    ISBN 0–948789–92–1 (paperback)

Acknowledgements

T
HE preparation of this book would not have been possible without the help and encouragement of so many people. I am most grateful to: the Longridge Local History Society for allowing me to reproduce, from its collection, many of the old photographs, and also to the members who have been liberal with their support and encouragement; Mr and Mrs A. Lord of Longridge for providing photographs and information relating to Queen's Mill; Mr T. Heginbotham for providing several of the photographs; North West Water for providing copies of documents concerning Alston College; Mr A. Lord of Chipping for loan of documents relating to Alston College and St John's College, Grimsargh; Mrs M. Lord of Chipping for researching the significance of the Birks datestone; Mr R. Wright for information on the Central Co-operative building; the Revd R. Awre, Vicar of Longridge, for allowing me to use material from the Alston Township Book; the staff of the Lancashire Record Office, who have searched out documents and granted permission for their use in this book; the staff of the Harris Reference Library who have, on so many occasions, carried the heavy bound volumes of the *Preston Pilot* up and down from the cellars; Dr A. Crosby for advising on the arrangement of the text, and also for supplying relevant historical information; the late Father Robert Coupe for drawing my attention to the historical importance of Newtown; my late wife, with whom I shared so many happy hours of research and discussion;and also, post- humously, to those who submitted to lengthy interviews from which reminiscences have been extracted. Most of all I must thank the people of Longridge and district, who have always been most kind and helpful in providing information and photographs, and allowing the examination of Deeds.

I hope I have succeeded in my aim of assembling much information which has not been previously published in book form. There are, of course, many aspects of Longridge history which have not been touched, but those must await further research.

Preface

I T is now over one hundred years since Tom Smith published his *History of Longridge*. It still remains the principal source book for the history of this area, and will probably continue to do so for some time. There are, however, several aspects which are not dealt with in that excellent volume, particularly those which relate to the second half of the nineteenth century and later, as they would not be considered to be 'history' by Smith, or they refer to events after the publication date. It has been my intention to fill in a few of the gaps. It is quite impossible to write about the history of Longridge without referring to Smith, but I have quoted him only where I felt it beneficial to do so in the context of my researches.

It must be made clear at the outset that a study of the history of Longridge really means a study of the ancient townships of Alston and Dilworth, for the present town sits astride the boundary between the two. Again, the townships of Whittingham and Thornley are so adjacent that they cannot be ignored, and neither can some of the other local townships, particularly when one is considering local conditions at a time when the village of Longridge was so small that specific examples from such a restricted area are not available. This accounts for my inclusion of documents from the mid seventeenth century (the civil war period) relating to the plight of individual women in the surrounding area, for surely there must have been many others in this area whose distress has not been so recorded.

Until the nineteenth century most written sources tended to be in the form of legal documents. The advent of newspapers provided a completely different form of written evidence – a source where fact, opinion and a certain amount of exaggeration combined under the pens of Victorian journalists, who rarely used a short word where a long one could be found. However, their obvious pleasure in the use of words is quite refreshing, particularly in their dramatic descriptions. Although there was no local newspaper for the Longridge area in the nineteenth century, reports from this locality appear sporadically in Preston papers. I have drawn heavily on those from the *Preston Pilot* when dealing with the period of great expansion in Longridge. In most cases I felt that a précis of the accounts would be quite inadequate, and so have preferred to quote in full the descriptions, lengthy though some of them are.

The importance of the railway in the development of Longridge can hardly be overstated. Factual and technical details of its construction and working are dealt with most adequately in Norman Parker's *The Preston and Longridge Railway*. I have taken the opportunity to use the observations of the journalists to describe the pleasures and the tragedies which accompanied the enterprise.

By using documents, newspaper reports and transcriptions of taped interviews I have tried to humanize events by showing how they affected actual people who lived hereabouts. This is not intended to be a chronological history, but rather a book about people in our history.

Contents

CHAPTER 1

Introduction

T HERE can be little doubt that the community which nestles at the south west end of the fell was named after the physical description of the feature – a long ridge. The first known documented reference to the village name appears in 1522,[1] but for a further three centuries the name was rather like a courtesy title as, officially or legally, precedence was given to the two townships of Alston and Dilworth which contain the village. Indeed, it is probable that prior to a date between 1450 and 1500 there was no village for which a name would be required.

As this area was so sparsely populated prior to 1500 it is useful to consider its history in a wider context than the immediate confines of the town. There is ample evidence that prehistoric peoples knew the ridge and its surroundings. Although such visible evidence in the immediate locality has not been discovered, it can be found within a short distance, proving that these ancient peoples lived, worked and died within a day's walk of here. Perhaps the best known of the local prehistoric sites is the Bleasdale Circle[2] set on slightly raised ground in a previously predominantly badly-drained area of land hemmed in by the sweeping arc of surrounding hills. The ritual site, in the form of a henge with a circle of wooden posts, must have drawn numbers of people to it both for the physical process of construction and later to a participate in the ritual activities associated with it. Such sites were not built by nomadic peoples, but by permanent residents of the area, and suggest a populace with a hierarchy which was able to organise the construction and use of the site. It is possible that burials found at the circle were those from that hierarchy.

Other prehistoric burial sites occur within a few miles. A burial cairn or tumulus[3] lies close to the River Ribble near to the old Boat House, opposite Hacking Hall, and a Neolithic burial cairn has been found at Slaidburn. These ancient peoples put much effort into their burial and ritual sites, and it is not surprising that these have stood the test of time much better than their dwelling- or work-places. However, bronze axes have been found in the Pilling area, along with a possible dwelling- or work-site on which was discovered a beautiful barbed and tanged flint arrowhead. A stone axehead was found near Longridge,[4] and recently one in the Bowland area. Although many flint tools have been found on the Rossendale hills, such artefacts have so far appeared only in small numbers on the Bowland, Bleasdale and Longridge fells.

One can imagine, therefore, that 4,000 years ago our locality was known and evaluated, by organised groups, for its usefulness or otherwise. As their dwelling sites have not been located it is not known whether any of their settlements were in this vicinity.

There is no doubt that the Romans knew the area well as it lies such a short distance from the fort at Ribchester. A road from the fort passes along the Ribble valley through Alston and on to Watling Street Road, Fulwood, and beyond to the Fylde. Another proceeds along Stoneygate Lane, past the Hall's Arms, and on to Jeffrey Hill before heading northwards to cross the Lune valley. A third passes close by Written Stone Farm in a north-westerly direction, but its further course is not certain. The ridge would have provided the Imperial army with an invaluable vantage point and they may well have established a lookout post near the south west end of the ridge from which to view the Vale of Chipping and also their route to the west.

Celtic head.
This Celtic head was built into the low wall at the side of the library in Barry Lane. Unfortunately, it was stolen.

After the departure of the Romans our land was coveted by the Vikings. Evidence of their presence is marked more by place names than by physical remains, although a Viking burial has been found at Claughton.[5] Notice that the ridge associated with Longridge is given the Norse name of 'fell'.

It was the Anglo-Saxon rulers of our country who, in the tenth and early eleventh centuries, organised, for tax purposes, a national system of administration by the formation of Hundreds or Wapentakes consisting of large areas of land each of which was divided into townships. This area lies within the Hundreds of Blackburn and Amounderness and within the Townships of Dilworth and Alston. Originally both were in Amounderness, but later Dilworth was transferred to Blackburn Hundred. The fact that the relevant townships are in two different Hundreds tends to complicate documentary research. Alston was frequently associated closely with the adjacent township of Hothersall so that they were referred to as Alston cum Hothersall. It is important to appreciate that there was no township of Longridge.

After gaining the throne, William I was anxious to acquire revenue and so he sent commissioners throughout the land to report on established customs and make assessments for taxation. The final report was compiled in 1086 and is now referred to as The Domesday Book.

Lancashire did not become a county until 1182, more than a century after the Norman Conquest. Domesday treated it as two separate entities: everything north of the Ribble was bundled in with Yorkshire, while the southern area 'between the Ribble and the Mersey' was considered a poor part of Cheshire. For the northern section Domesday does little more than list the names of settlements. In the hundred known as Amounderness (which then included Alston and Dilworth) sixty-two settlements are mentioned. Of these, says Domesday, sixteen 'have a few inhabitants . . . the rest are waste'. The term 'waste' still puzzles historians. Was it caused by William, who after suppressing rebellions in Yorkshire in 1069–70 moved west through the hills so as to overrun Amounderness and treat it with the utmost severity? Or was

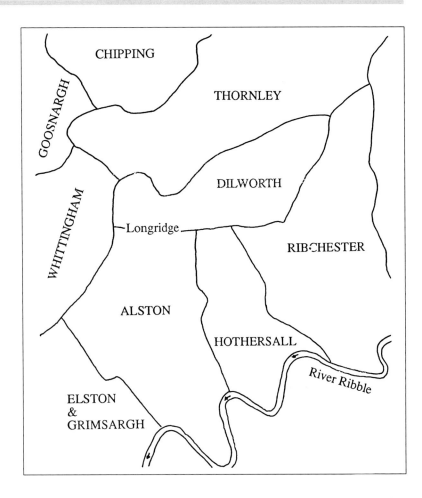

Local townships.

it considered 'waste' because the commissioners from the south considered land as such which was not suitable for arable farming. Or was the area so inhospitable at this northern extremity of England that the commissioners preferred to give it but scant attention and return south as soon as possible?

Before the conquest the area was held by Earl Tostig, Harold Godwinson's traitorous brother. It was Tostig's collaboration with the King of Norway to oust Harold from the Saxon throne that led to Harold's march to victory at Stamford Bridge followed by his forced march to defeat at Hastings in 1066. After the conquest all the area was given to, or held by, Roger de Poictou. Later it passed to the De Lacey's who built Clitheroe Castle. Their principal castle was at Pontefract.

In our area the Domesday survey records a township called 'Actun'.[6] At the time that Smith wrote his *History of Longridge* (1888) this was thought to refer to Alston[7] – 'Athel's ton', meaning the settlement named after Athelstan, the tenth-century Saxon king who won a battle in the vicinity. Now historians tend to think that Actun is probably Aighton.[8] Domesday records a township of 'Bileuurde' which is now thought to be Dilworth.[9] Smith suggests that the name Dilworth is derived from 'dil' – an idol, and 'worth'[10] – an enclosure, hence 'enclosure of idols'. Now it is thought more likely to mean an enclosure where dill was grown; a plant used for medicinal and cooking purposes. However there is still an element of uncertainty in the derivations of the names.

Long ago there was no standardised spelling and names were usually spelt as spoken, often in local dialect. Tom Smith gives quite a list of variations. Dilworth[11] has had many variations – Dylleword, Dilword (a final 'd' in Old English was pronounced like the present 'th' – compare with the Welsh 'dd' which is also pronounced as 'th'), Dylleworth, Dileworthe. Longridge is recorded as Longryche, Longerydche, Langrigg, Langridge and Langrytch.[12]

Throughout the Middle Ages several families assumed ownership of parts of the area. Smith records that they included the de Hodreshalls, de Hoghtons, de Singletons, de Alstons.[13] A small part of Dilworth was owned by Cockersand Abbey. From the sixteenth century the Lords of the Manor have been the Hothersalls, Singletons, de Hoghtons, Stratberrells, Leckonbys and Crosses. Much land has also been owned by the Radcliffes, Cottams, Nelsons and the Earls of Derby.

It is common for villages to bear the name of the township in which they are situated, but there has never been a historical township of Longridge. One might ask why, then, was the village not called Alston or Dilworth? In order to understand the reason for the naming of the settlement one must go back perhaps 500 years and consider the ecclesiastical parish of Ribchester. The church of St Wilfrid was originally established to serve the scattered communities in the five townships of Ribchester, Dutton, Dilworth, Alston and Hothersall. It was to the church at Ribchester that the people of the townships were obliged to go for all services, christenings, marriages and funerals. Most people at that time would travel on foot and for those at the extremities of Alston and Dilworth this could be physically taxing as well as time consuming. Many older people would find the journey almost impossible. In order to make it easier for the inhabitants of Alston and Dilworth to attend church, a chapel-of-ease dedicated to St Lawrence was built close to the boundary between the two townships which it was intended to serve. The date of construction is not known, but the first known documentary reference occurs in 1522 in the rental of the Earl of Derby's estates: '4d. of a new rent of a parcel of land from the lord's waste near the chapel of Longerygge containing ½ rood of land enclosed by Richard Fairclough'.

Although an exact date for the foundation of the chapel is not known it is probable that this occurred between 1450 and 1500. From that time this chapel at the south-west end of the ridge would act as the focal point close to which cottages would be built. Thus a community was established around the chapel and up the fell road. In these circumstances it would have been inappropriate to name it after either township and so it took on the name of the ridge which supported it.

CHAPTER 2

The Chapel and its Village

The Church of St Lawrence

REFERENCE to the establishment of this chapel-of-ease has been made earlier. As the chapel or church of a community, particularly in the past, played such an important part in the life of the people its history is very relevant to a history of the area. The earliest record of a priest is in 1554:[1]'Sir Robert Cotome, priest of Longryche in Ribblechester.' It was usual at that time to bestow the title 'Sir' on the parish priest. It was said of Sir Robert that, 'he was grave and chaste, could play on the musiques, and was noe typler nor dyce man'.[2]

One of his successors, a century later, deserves mention. It is recorded that in 1662 Timothy Smith was 'ejected'. What was his crime? During the commonwealth period many of the clergy considered preaching of primary importance, as adherence to the rituals of the Church of England was no longer necessary. After the restoration of the monarchy the Church of England was re-established; parliament considered this rise in Presbyterianism a dangerous practice and to combat it passed the Act of Uniformity in 1662, which imposed strict adherence to the Book of Common Prayer and insisted that all clergy take an oath of compliance. The Act was very unpopular, and a great number refused to comply and were forced to give up their livings. One such priest was Timothy Smith of Longridge Chapel who was, therefore, ejected. It would appear, however, that it was difficult to monitor the situation as Smith continued to preach in the chapel and later became known as a leading nonconformist at Longridge. Indeed in 1672 Timothy Smith's house was licensed for the Presbyterians.

It was not until 1664 and the Conventicle Act that legal measures were taken to suppress dissenting congregations in churches, a conventicle being an illegal religious gathering. Presumably, however, such gatherings continued for, in 1676, the Quarter Sessions at Preston had to deal with 'The Conventicle of James Hartley'.[3] There seems to have been a 'tip off', for Alexander Nowell, a justice of the peace, personally appeared in Longridge to witness one James Hartley 'preachinge at ye Chappell contrary to an act of parliament . . . for supporting siditious conventicles where there was assembled above forty persons in number and y^t they were preaching

This painting shows that the boundary wall between the inn and the churchyard actually butts onto the tower. Entry via the tower door must have been through the inn yard. The door in the south porch was built up in about 1926 and the porch made into the baptistry.

For many years five cottages shared the 'island' with the church and the Duke William. The cottages, on the right, were demolished in 1926. The road was closed so that the graveyard could be extended.

contrary to ye practice of ye Liturgy of ye Church of England'. It was not thought necessary to bring the whole congregation before the Court, but, presumably to set an example, a gentleman, one John Whittingham, was singled out for attention by the Sessions.

It would appear that throughout the sixteenth and seventeenth centuries this was a parochial chapelry of a poor district. To make matters worse for long periods the chapel had no minister, which was hardly surprising as there was no endowment before 1735 even though the district contained at least

The parish church in 1893. A major renovation took place in 1900. The lych gate was erected in 1939. The clock came from Alston College, a boarding school demolished when the nearby reservoir was constructed.

140 families.[4] After 1735 the purchase of land and farms in Goosnargh and Preston provided the endowment which was so desperately needed.

Whilst the date of its foundation is not known dates of rebuilding in 1716, 1784, 1822 and 1900 are documented. The tower was added in 1841. In the past the running costs of the chapel were met by the inhabitants of the two townships of Alston and Dilworth. Dilworth paid one third and Alston two thirds,[5] probably because of the ratio of their populations long ago. Originally the chapel stood in the centre of an 'island' with a road running completely round it. Also on the island on the south side was the earliest recorded school in Longridge. A plaque set in the wall opposite the row of cottages states: 'A school erected by privat contributions for the publick good, 1731'. This school was replaced in 1832 when a new one was built close by on the opposite side of the chapel. It is now a joiner/undertaker's shop, but still retains its datestone, MDCCCXXXII. Also sharing the island with the chapel were five cottages and the Duke William.

An early painting of the south side of the church shows that the boundary wall between the Duke and the churchyard actually butted onto the church tower, in which case entry via the tower door could only have been made through the yard of the inn. The back of the inn came to within fifteen feet of the tower. However, an alternative entry to the church could be made through a door in the south porch, and this can clearly be seen in the painting. The south porch no longer has a door and is used as a baptistry.

This early Duke William was probably built in the mid eighteenth century and was demolished about 1880. Its removal allowed an extension of the burial area and also improved the general aspect of the site. It also provided one man, who was born in the old inn, with the rare distinction of being buried on the same spot. After the Duke William was demolished a new inn

was built across the road on the site of the present one. After the cottages were demolished about 1926 the graveyard was extended across part of the road which had for so long surrounded the chapel site.

During the eighteenth century the affairs of the local community were controlled by a body called the select vestry. Although today this name may suggest an exclusively church body, this was certainly not so 200 years ago. The vestry was, in fact, the eighteenth-century equivalent of today's parish council. The select vestry for Alston met at the White Bull in Alston, whilst that for Dilworth met at the White Bull in Dilworth. There were twelve to fourteen men in each of these groups, most of them being local farmers. Each year they appointed four principal officers – the overseer of the poor, the overseer of the highways, the constable and the chapel- or churchwarden. Each of the four officials collected money for his particular purpose from the householders in the community. This was the equivalent of what was until recently the rates. The vestry established the rate of the contribution, which was then referred to the justices of the peace for approval. It is, therefore, clear that the affairs of the chapel were very closely involved in the civil administration. Indeed it was the duty of the whole community to support the chapel even though many of the individuals would have differing religious views.

The old Duke William stood immediately in front of the church tower. It was demolished about 1880. One man was born there, and is buried on the same spot.

*The school opposite the
church, built in 1832 and
closed in 1885.*

The churchwardens' accounts for that period itemise many day to day
running expenses incurred in maintaining the chapel.[6] Bell ropes, costing
1s. 6d. (7p) needed replacement at regular intervals. In 1776 the old Bible
was exchanged for a new one at a cost of 11s. 6d. (57p). Six years later it
was repaired for 5s. 8d. (28p). Surplices were washed regularly at an annual
cost of 1s. 6d. (7p). The roof of the chapel at that time would be stone slate
as references are made to the supplying of slate and the repairs carried out
by John Fletcher, usually for about 1s. 6d. (7p). The interior walls would be
plastered and lime washed. From time to time wheat straw was bought. This
was scattered on the floor. As late as 1837 a document stated: 'The Clerk
shall remove the straw from the floor and lay down fresh straw when
required by the Chapelwardens'. This practice stopped about 1845. In 1895
the parish church floor was covered with linoleum by Miss Wright as 'it
gives warmth and quietness which were wanting before'. Musical accom-
paniment was by instrumentalists.[7] Bassoon reeds were bought for 3s. 4d.
(17p).[8] In 1794 the vestry of Ribchester decided to give a new 'Bazoon' and
'Hautboy' (a wooden double reeded wind instrument of high pitch) to the
Chapel of Longridge. In 1847 it is recorded that 'Old Bob Booth played a
bassoon while William Eaves played the big fiddle, and W. Rhodes manipu-
lated the clarionet'.[9]

It would appear, however, that all was not sweetness and harmony especially when obstreperous members of the congregation were present, for
example in 1782: 'Pade to George Cluff for kepin Lundun Jack fro distorbin
t'kongrgation at chappel, 7 pence, for being crazd. (signed) J.S.'.[10]

George Ratcliffe was chapelwarden in 1784 when the chapel was repaired.[11] The total cost of 'repairing and Inlarging Longridge Chappel' was
£123 7s. 4¾d. Voluntary donations or subscriptions amounted to £45 2s. 6d.

The waterhead on the old parsonage. The initials are those of Robert Parkinson and his wife.

In the course of his normal duties Ratcliffe collected £44 12s. 0d. in Alston, whilst Dilworth contributed £26 1s. 7½d. There was £3 0s. 5½d. left in the warden's account from the previous year. Today all this seems reasonable, but we may now be surprised to note that a further £2 16s. 0d. came from the overseer of the poor and 4s. 11d. from the constable's account. This was surplus money from the previous year. The above illustrates the link between church and community whereby the select vestry had an important responsibility for the upkeep of the chapel. There was clearly a celebratory service, with an augmented choir, held at the conclusion of the work for 10s. 6d. was 'Given Longridge & Lango singers for their expence at opening the Chappell'. The parson, the Rev. Robert Parkinson, incurred expenses of 1s. 8d. Although it is not recorded in the Alston Township Book a new parsonage was built in 1786. This very fine house still stands in Market Place (opposite Kestor Lane). A waterhead bears the date and Rev. Parkinson's initials and those of his wife. This gentleman was also closely associated with the building of Club Row in the late 1790s. He acted as Chairman of the 'Club'. The parsonage was sold in 1846 and a new vicarage built in Lower Lane in the same year.

In 1837 the Vicar of Ribchester consented to the solemnization of matrimony in the chapel, providing that at least one of the parties resided in Alston or Dilworth.[12] The following newspaper report on 26 May 1838 confirms the above agreement:[13]

MARRIAGE at Longridge Chapel by Rev. Maude –
Mr James Bond of Knowle Green to Miss Elizabeth Jump of Dilworth.
This is the first time a marriage has been solemnised in this place of worship.

An old inhabitant told Tom Smith that she remembered occasions in the early 1800s when the churchwardens, in addition to their church duties, used to visit public houses on Sundays in order to detect illicit drinking. Any publicans and clients caught were fined for 'chapel breaking', as it was called. This could well have been a response to an official notice in 1829 from the justices of the peace to the constables, churchwardens and overseers of the poor of Alston. They were informed that they should strictly and diligently search out and apprehend all persons practising 'Leaping, Playing at Football, Quoits, Bowls, and many other unlawful games; Hunting Tippling in the Ale-houses, Swearing, Cursing, Profaning the Sabbath, and absenting themselves in time of Divine Service from the Church on the Lord's Day'. Any persons guilty of such conduct were rendered liable to the penalty of 'Three shillings and Fourpence, for the use of the poor in the Township where such offences were committed, or sit in the Stocks for the space of three hours'. The village stocks used to be placed in the south-east portion of the churchyard. Drunkards were most often found in them.[14]

During the nineteenth century the chapel played an active and central role in the annual celebrations of various local societies. Each Whit Monday saw processions by the Sick Societies of Longridge. There seem to have been three principal ones – the Sunday School Sick Society, the Old Brotherly Society and the Roman Catholic Benefit Club. The first two processed to St Lawrence's where either the incumbent or a guest delivered an appropriate sermon after which the seniors returned in procession to the Red Lion for an 'excellent dinner'. The youngsters were entertained in the 'New School Rooms' (now the joiner/undertaker's shop) with pies, currant buns and ginger beer. The Roman Catholics processed to Alston Lane Church and then repaired to either the Duke William or the White Bull in Alston for ample refreshment. The *Preston Pilot* described the scene thus:[15]

The females were attired in their best summer dresses, and the spirit of rivalry had attained its highest pitch, for all appeared so happy that, save the ambition of everyone endeavouring to outvie her companion in neatness of appearance, one could only have had an idea of one mass of beauty and gracefulness. Next followed the males – a jovial regiment, from the little fellow just put into jacket and trowsers, to the more manly youth, with his best coat and hat, and ruddy face – his flower tucked in his buttonhole, and his glances before him at the pretty country girl. Having entered the church in the best possible order attended by their faithful teachers, the scholars and the whole congregation had a sermon preached by their newly appointed and highly respected minister, Rev. J. Pigot, M.A. whose pastoral visits to the sick and others have been most active and exemplary.

Longridge Guild was held in August each year. This was the occasion for the colourful processions of the schools and friendly societies followed by their attendance at a church service. The Sunday scholars, carrying the handsome banner of the Sick Society, led the way accompanied by the

Longridge Brass Band. The girls' school and the boys' school followed with the school banner and Barton's Brass Band. Then came the guilds, attired in sashes, rosettes and bearing regalia, marching in an order which had been determined by ballot. First The Order of Druids, headed by two men on horseback, dressed in the costume of the Ancient Druids; second The Grand United Order of Oddfellows; third The Order of Mechanics and fourth The Independent Order of Oddfellows. In earlier years they were joined by The Female Charitable Sick Society. The procession marched up Berry Lane, along King Street, High Street as far as Cut Thorn Row, then doubled and returned by way of Market Place, Fell Brow, Little Lane, Kestor Lane, Pitt Street, as far as the Bone Mill and doubling there proceeded to their respective schools and lodges. (The Corn & Bone Mill was on the site of the present dairy. Pitt Street stretched from Stone Bridge to the Alston Arms.) The children were served with buns and coffee whilst the guild members, whose lodges met at various inns, were able to partake of a 'capital dinner' which awaited them. The chapel or church incumbent was president of both Orders of Oddfellows and attended their dinners alternately.

There were seven principal friendly societies established in Longridge during the nineteenth century. The 'No Danger' Lodge of the Independent Order of Oddfellows was formed in 1840 and met at the White Lion Inn, Hothersall (opposite the present Corporation Arms), and later at the Dog Inn; followed by the United Order of Catholic Brethren, Alston District in 1844 at the White Bull, Alston; the 'St Lawrence' Lodge of the Grand United Order of Oddfellows in 1850 at the White Bull, Dilworth; the Ancient Order of Druids in 1852; the Longridge Independent Sick and Funeral Society in 1867; the Mechanics Club in 1874; and the Independent Order of Rechabites in 1881.

The growth of industry in Longridge in the second half of the nineteenth century naturally led to a vast increase in the population. This increase had an important effect on the status of the chapel. No longer was it reasonable for it to remain a chapel-of-ease, and so, in 1868, the Ecclesiastical Parish of Longridge was established and the chapel became the parish church.

Early Parish Registers

ALSTON and Dilworth were part of Ribchester Ecclesiastical Parish until 1868. This meant that parish records relating to the inhabitants of these two townships were entered in the Ribchester parish register.

Since 1538, during the reign of Henry VIII, every parish had to keep records of christenings, marriages and burials. These were entered in a register. From 1597, during the reign of Elizabeth I, the entries were copied, from time to time, and sent to the Diocesan Registry as bishop's transcripts. The production of two identical lists would appear to be an excellent method of record keeping, but it had serious drawbacks. Many registers were carelessly written up or were carelessly copied. Many entries were illegible

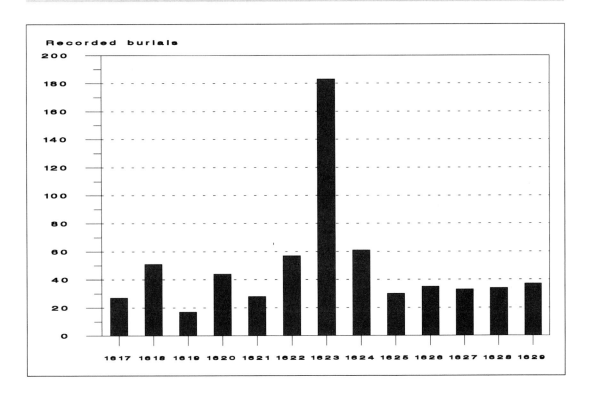

Recorded burials in Ribchester Parish Register 1617–29

and many seem to have been written from memory from time to time. The earliest surviving Ribchester parish register dates from 1598.

It is not surprising, therefore, that the Ribchester records display many of the above shortcomings by omissions or irregularities in the sequence of entries.[16] A confident start was made in 1598 with twenty-two christenings, four burials, but strangely no marriages. Whilst christenings and burials seem to have been recorded with some consistency for five years the same cannot be said for marriages – nine in 1599, none in 1600, but twenty-one in 1601 and back to none in 1602. Why was Cupid so active in 1601, but absent in the years either side? Entries are sparse and spasmodic from 1603 to 1616 at which time burials, at least, seem to be recorded again with more consistency. From 1620 to 1640 a credible number of entries were made. During the Civil War and the early years of the commonwealth period entries virtually cease. Records of christenings and burials begin again in 1653, but it is 1660 before another marriage is recorded. Thereafter the entries appear more reliable because of their consistency.

The inconsistency and irregularity of the records mean that they are of little value for demographic purposes. Also it must be remembered that christenings cannot necessarily be equated with births. Despite all these drawbacks some historical (as well as genealogical) use can be made of the register. Fortunately the incumbent or clerk did refer to many people as being from Alston, Dilworth or Hothersall, which is most helpful.

Perhaps the most striking, but poignant, entries occur in 1623 when death stalked the area and left its mark in so many households. The average burial rate for the parish of thirty-four per year was dwarfed by a massive 183 in 1623 as an epidemic struck with the utmost severity. Of these, twenty-nine are recorded as living in Alston or Dilworth. In order to appreciate the significance of this number a similar ratio today would mean over 300 deaths in Longridge. The cause of this epidemic is now thought to have been famine combined with disease consequent upon malnutrition. At this time a similar situation occurred throughout the north of England.

The Fairclough family of Alston Lane suffered several mortalities: on 12 January, Robert buried two of his children; on 5 June, Janet, probably an older child, was buried; and finally, on 29 September, Robert himself was laid to rest. William Rudley was buried on 6 May followed by one of his children on 10 September. Alice Dolphin of Ward Green and her child were buried on 4 November. Thomas Twogood lost two children, whilst James Cottam of Dilworth buried both his wife and a child. The scourge claimed a high proportion of its victims from the young as almost half the burials were of children.

Infant mortality was very high. The records are littered with references to the christening of children followed by their burials within a few days or months. Sadly many mothers were buried within days of the christening of a child. Childbirth was decidedly dangerous. A high birth rate was necessary to counteract the high death rate. In 1683 there are sixteen recorded burials, of which twelve were of children.

Unfortunately there is little correlation between the christening and burial lists. Ideally one would like to be able to link a christening with a later burial, particularly as there was little movement of population at that time, but this is possible only in a minority of cases. In the register there tend to be more burials recorded than christenings. For example in the twenty-year period from 1680 to 1699 there are eighty-two christenings, but 200 burials. This would suggest a rapid fall in the population of Alston and Dilworth, but this was not so. One must assume that either many christenings were not recorded, or that many children were not baptized, or, as this was a strongly Catholic area, many were secretly baptized in that faith. However, most would be buried at the parish church. One entry reads: '1684 Richard ye son of John Billington of Dillworth Clandestine'. Whilst most christenings took place at Ribchester the earliest references to ones taking place locally read:

1683 12th August Anne ye d. of Richard Wallton of Allston Christend at Longridge
1684 Thomas ye son of Richard Slater of Alston Church at Chapell

The earliest local burial is recorded in 1702: '1702 12 Jan Rich: Parkinson in Longridge Chaple in Als'.

During the reign of Elizabeth I a law was passed which stipulated that corpses should be wrapped in woollen cloth for burial. This was intended to boost the woollen trade. Although this law lapsed in the seventeenth century an entry reads: '1678 7 Sept Widow Seed in Dillworth in woolen'.

From time to time references are made to illegitimate births, for example:

1635 21 July Mary the d. of Robt: Radcliffe in Dillworth bastard
1701 23 Feb John ye son of Mary Greenal Ilegit de Hoth

An unmarried mother and child presented a problem for the overseer as such a family would usually need financial support. Where it was possible to name the father of the child the overseer presented a petition to the Quarter Sessions in order to obtain a contribution towards maintenance of the child.

Thus in April 1732 the following judgement[17] was made in the case of Mary Keighley, singlewoman, who

> was on the fifteenth day of March last past delivered of a male bastard child since Christened James in the Townshipp of Alston cum Hothersall af[ore]s[ai]d and in the parish of Ribchester in the s[ai]d County of Lancaster is now being and is likely to become chargable to the s[ai]d Townshipp of Alston cum Hothersall And . . . it appeareth that John Parkinson of Goosnargh in the County of Lancaster Carpenter is the father of the sd bastard child

Two magistrates determined that John Parkinson should

> pay weekly and every week from the time of the birth of the sd bastard child and for so long as it shall be chargable to the sd Townshipp of Alston cum Hothersall unto the Churchwardens or Overseers . . .the sum of ten pence for and towards the maintenance and bringing up of the sd bastard child and also to pay the sd Churchwardens or Overseers of the Poor . . . upon notice of this our Order the sum of ten shillings expended and laid out by the sd Overseers for the sd Mary Keighley during her lying in childbed

Mary was also ordered to pay fourpence a week for the upkeep of the child.

Several other entries over the years for this locality are worthy of note:

1659 29 August 2 children of Thomas Hille in Dillworth being murthred
1697 2 June yn was found a childe in a pound in Huthersal neare ffransas Green with its mouth stopt full of rags suposed to be ye childe of Anne Radcliffe widow
1710 18 February Geo: Preston de Dill by a wishbone
1719 12 August Jeremiah Page de Dill Husbandman
Joseph son of ye sd Jeremiah Page strangled himself August 9th all night.

One cannot begin to imagine the agonies suffered by Anne Radcliffe. Perhaps the recent loss of her husband still weighed heavily on her mind. At that time widowhood was particularly difficult with little opportunity for work especially with young children. Support from Poor Relief was minimal.

Joseph Page was a young man of twenty-one years (christened 6 March 1698) when he committed suicide. The loss of his parents probably weighed heavily on his mind for his mother had died the previous year.

Fees, of course, had to be paid for burials. Many of the dead did not have sufficient means and so it was left to the overseer of the poor to meet the cost:

1705 18 July James Seed de Dill: musishon per overseer aged 66
1706 10 Dec Jno: Horn de Dill: poor laborer per overseer
1706 13 Dec Rich: Duckworth de Dill: per overseer

Destitute vagrants or travellers were not welcome in townships as they were a burden for the overseer who had to take responsibility for them. If he or the constable could move them on so much the better.

1700 18 Feb a child of a poor traveler by ye overseer de Als
1703 31 Jan Mary Livesey a traveler woman who died in Als

No doubt most corpses were carried with dignity from all parts of the parish to their last resting place. However special note is made of the mode of transport of one poor inhabitant of Alston whose neighbours did what they could: '1626 26 ffebruary A poore man foorth of Allston wch was borne on a barrowe'.

A grim reminder of the 1715 Jacobite Rebellion occurs in two entries:

1716 Oct 3 Jon Winckley de Alst Executed for Treason
Oct 3 Tho: Shutlworth de Alst Executed for Treason

Most local Jacobite supporters were Roman Catholics, as probably were these two. One wonders where their execution took place. Perhaps it was, with many others, at Gallows Hill on the outskirts of Preston, close to the present English Martyrs Church. There, in the names of streets, are recalled the more illustrious rebels, Derwentwater and Kenmure, who were also executed, but in their cases in London.

CHAPTER 3

Some Interesting Properties

T HE previous chapter has referred to many events in the locality during
the seventeenth and eighteenth centuries. Whilst the people involved
are no longer with us some of the houses which were scattered about
the neighbourhood at the time still are. If only walls could speak what stories
they could tell!

Hacking Hobs, Alston

THE name is quite intriguing and no satisfactory explanation can be pro-
vided. The first part of the name is repeated in other parts of the locality. In
Dilworth, on the Knowle Green road, there was a house called Hacking
Wifes, and at the confluence of the Ribble and the Calder sits Hacking Hall.
The second part can be spelt with either one or two 'b's. A document of 1673
refers to the farm as the 'Platt at the Hobbs'(a platt being a bridge).

   The house is of early seventeenth-century (1608) origin and has been
extensively altered over the years. Remnants of mullioned windows and drip
moulds no doubt belonged to the original building. These have been replaced
by larger windows. The roof space is particularly interesting for it reveals
more of the past history of the house. During one of the periods when the
internal design was changed the purlins were raised in order to make the
pitch of the roof less steep and give more headroom on the first floor. An
oak spiral staircase leads from the first floor into the roof space. A niche in
the wall would have held a candle to light the way. Much of the roof space
was lime washed with a small window in the gable giving a small amount
of light. This was probably a garret used by the servants. The census of 1861
reveals that a fifteen-year-old farm boy and an eleven-year-old general
servant girl were living in the house.

   A number of years ago the gable end of the barn showed clearly the
remains of a mullioned window and the outline in the stonework of a gable
of much smaller proportions. As the window was placed symmetrically
inside the smaller gable there is a strong possibility that the barn was
extended around a small cottage which was earlier used by a farm labourer.
In this area the grouping of farms and cottages into folds was very common.

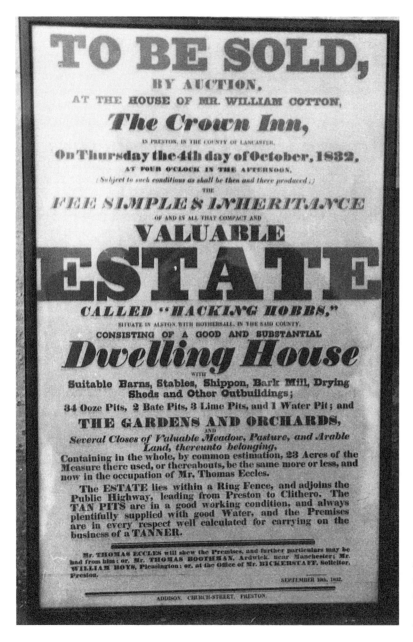

A poster from 1832 advertising the sale of the Hacking Hobbs estate. (Photograph courtesy of Mrs M. Roberts.)

A cursory look at a map reveals Bolton Fold, Walton Fold, Sharley Fold, Nook Fold, etc.

The extent of the farm land seems to have fluctuated considerably. When the farm was sold in 1832 it had twenty-three acres, the 1851 census puts it down to nine acres, but up to forty-seven acres in 1871. Much of the early wealth came from tanning. Reference to this is made in more detail in

Chapter 8 (Newtown). At the sale of 1832 there were thirty-two ooze pits, two bate pits, three lime pits and one water pit all used in the tanning process. The practice of processing each hide separately would account for the large number of pits. In common with many of the farms in the area there was a well and pump on the premises which would account for the farm having 'a plentiful supply of water'.

The following intriguing entry appeared in the *Lancashire Daily Post* in January 1936:

NOAH'S ARK TRAIN LEAVES LONGRIDGE
Farm Removed to Wiltshire

Resembling a Noah's Ark, a train left Longridge this afternoon for High-worth, near Swindon, a distance of two hundred miles.

It comprised of [sic] eleven trucks of livestock and thirteen of farm implements and sectional cabins and practically the whole of the farm stock of Hacking Hobs farm, Longridge, the property of Mrs Kate Hollas, of Red Scar, Grimsargh, near Preston.

Mrs Hollas has taken up Parsonage Farm, Highworth, following the sale of Red Scar to Messrs Courtaulds. There were on the train six shires, a hunter and two foals, a Shetland pony, forty five sheep, a bull, fifteen cows, twenty seven stirks, eighteen yearlings and four calves. The farm implements included carts, traps, ploughs, harrows, turnip cutter, harness and feeding utensils.

The cows were milked before leaving and will be at Parsonage Farm in time for early morning milking and by 9 a.m. tomorrow it is expected that the whole of the livestock will have been safely transported and will be grazing in the fields of Wiltshire.

Apparently the only member of her household she did not take was her husband. Mr Hollas moved to Lytham St Annes. The journey was done in reverse about 1939 when Mrs Hollas came back north to farm at Hothersall Hall. One wonders whether such a journey could be undertaken by rail now. It was, of course, a great advantage to have the railway line so close to the farm at that time.

Crumpax, Dilworth

CRUMPAX farmhouse bears the oldest datestone in Longridge – 1596. The name itself is interesting as it appears to be a variation of 'Crampoaks'. 'Cramp' is a word which has a meaning of 'compressed' or 'bent'. There is no doubt that the low-lying land close by was very wet and marshy long ago and was only turned into useful agricultural fields by extensive draining in the early part of the nineteenth century. Attempts to work the land in the sixteenth century would have been hampered by the presence of buried trunks and branches of oak trees which had once grown in this area. Hundreds of years of lying buried in such wet conditions produced a wood called bog oak. Bog oak is extremely hard and may have given the impression of being compressed or 'cramped', and added to this feature is the fact that oak does produce bent or gnarled branches. Perhaps that is the origin of the name.

The house itself has been extensively altered over the years and apart from the datestone gives little external evidence of its age. However it is not many years since a section of wattle and daub wall was removed from inside. The wattle had vertical oak staves which were interwoven with thin hazel branches. This frame was then packed and surrounded by a thick layer of daub. Many of the roof timbers are probably original. They are of oak and are far from straight. The ceilings pre-date the use of laths and were made from reeds onto which the plaster was pressed and spread.

Berry's Farm, Alston

BEHIND the Alston reservoirs lies this most interesting house. It was probably built early in the seventeenth century, or perhaps even earlier, and was originally a single-bay cruck-framed thatched dwelling. Its lands were never extensive and so its owners or occupiers were not as prosperous as those who replaced their houses early in the seventeenth century. However, in common with several other farms, it was found possible to modernise the house in the second half of the eighteenth century when farming was more profitable. Unlike so many of the farmhouse alterations it was decided, perhaps for financial reasons, to retain the crucks and to concentrate on rebuilding the outer walls, raising them in height to accommodate a stone slate roof of shallower pitch, and giving additional headroom upstairs. At the same time the mullioned windows were replaced and the whole building was extended at one end. The outer walls of the house were rendered until a few years ago. When this material was removed the gable end revealed the original steep pitch required by the thatch. A small section of a blocked mullioned window was built into the front wall, but it may not be in its original position.

Chapel Brow, Alston

MOST of the cottages in and around Longridge would be built in a less substantial way than the farmhouses and few, if any of them, have survived. They have been demolished and replaced by newer houses. Some of the earliest properties in Longridge would be built near to the chapel of St Lawrence as it was usual for a church to be the focal point of a village. It is not surprising, therefore, to find two cottages on Chapel Brow which show strong evidence of seventeenth-century construction. The two houses have front and rear façades which are not contemporary with each other – a sure sign of rebuilding. As it was not normal at that time to build semi-detached houses one must assume that this was originally one house. On the ground floor at the rear are the remains of a pair of seventeenth-century three-light windows with cavetto (concave) mullions. Later, in the eighteenth or early nineteenth century, the house was altered in a way similar to Birks or Berry's farmhouses. The front façade was completely rebuilt with new windows, a raised wall height and contemporary eaves construction. Work at the back, though, was restricted to raising the wall height and inserting new upper windows. The original house probably had a stone flagged roof as some roofing flags have been unearthed in the garden. The house was probably divided at the time of the reconstruction.

Old Dun Cow Rib, Whittingham

THIS farmhouse, better known as Th'Owd Rib, is situated in Halfpenny Lane on the outskirts of Longridge. This lane was probably a drovers' route long ago. The cattle drovers used to halt their herds for the night at recognised places, often just outside villages where refreshment or supplies could be obtained. It was usual at such places for a charge to be made to compensate for the overnight consumption of herbage by the animals. The toll is reflected in the name of the lane.

The house itself was built in 1616 by Adam Hoghton; his initials, the date and the Hoghton arms are carved above the doorway. At the time of building the property was called Moor Farm. This name provides a reminder that at

Old Dun Cow Rib, built by Adam Hoghton in 1616 and named Moor Farm. This photograph was taken before the lean-to on the left was demolished and the house extended. The rib above the door and the projecting toilet on the gable-end can be seen.

21

the beginning of the seventeenth century there was probably an area of unfenced moorland stretching between Longridge and Goosnargh. The drovers would pass along the edge of this moorland. At a later date the house came to be associated with the legend which resulted in its present unusual name.

Apparently a time of drought and famine in the area had brought the local folk to a low ebb of health. It was then that a dun-coloured cow wandered the lanes and allowed each cottager to fill a vessel with milk. This benevolent beast thus sustained the local populace, but its actions did not meet with the approval of the local witch, who milked the cow into a sieve. Try as it could the animal could not fill the vessel. Its efforts to do so resulted in its untimely death. The distraught people carefully buried the body, some say at Cow Hill, Grimsargh. One of its ribs was removed and placed above the doorway of the farmhouse as a reminder of the life-saving action of this most unusual animal. The rib remains in position to this day.

It must be said that the above legend is not unique to this area. A precisely similar one exists in Shropshire. There the witch and her family were punished for her wicked deed; she and her daughters were turned into pillars of stone. They all remain to this day as the Mitchell Fold Stone Circle.

The front of the house presents a typical early seventeenth-century façade. It has mullioned windows with drip moulds and a stone flagged roof to the front. Originally the house was smaller. It has been extended at the opposite end to the front door. Round the corner from the door, on the gable end, there is a small projecting room with an overhang. This was a lavatory with a hole in the floor of the overhang – a logical development from the garderobes found in castles in former times.

Birks, Thornley

THE farmhouse now known as Birks used to be called Higher Birks for across the road from it was another farmhouse called Lower Birks. This has been demolished, but its farm buildings remain in use. 'Birks' means 'birches' so presumably there must have been several of these trees in the vicinity. Birks is now situated on a quiet road running from the fell road down into Thornley. Many years ago this was the main route from Longridge to Chipping and avoided the lower marshy ground. It lost its status as a principal route when improved drainage made possible the construction of a road past the Alston Arms. In its heyday Birks was important, for it was an inn used by those travelling to and from Chipping. Today the house displays two contrasting styles of architecture resulting from a rebuilding of the front façade. The rear of the house retains early seventeenth-century mullioned windows of the original construction. In common with many farms in the area, a period of prosperity in the first half of the eighteenth century led to modernisation of the farmhouses in the second half. At Birks the entire front façade was replaced and the interior altered. Parts of the mullioned front windows were then used to frame the remodelled tall stair window at the rear.

It is fortunate that a very detailed inventory of the contents of the house and the farm equipment and livestock, dated 1663, has survived. In it there is reference to items stored in Oaks Barn. That very same barn still survives in an adjacent field. Initially it was of cruck construction, part of which still remains.

In August 1990 a datestone was found above the door at the rear of the house:

$$
\begin{array}{cc}
& S \\
1616 & R\ E
\end{array}
$$

The date of 1616 is consistent with the mullioned windows at the back of the house, and is, therefore, probably the date of building of the house. The front façade was completely remodelled in the second half of the eighteenth century.The initials refer to a husband, R.S., and his wife E.S. The Sowerbutts owned Birks at that time. A will of 1592 refers to 'Thomas Sowerbutts of Byrks, yeoman'. The Chipping parish register records the marriage in 1612 of Richard Sowerbutts and Elizabeth Breadley (Bradley). There is a strong possibility that the initials are those of these two people. Elizabeth probably lived at the neighbouring farm, still called Bradleys.

Probate Inventories

HAVING discussed several seventeenth-century or earlier farmhouses in the immediate area, one may wonder what living conditions were like in those houses 300 years ago. Fortunately there are surviving documents which do help provide some answers; these are referred to as probate inventories.

Henry VIII ordained that wills should be proved in an ecclesiastical court. He also required that before probate could be granted an inventory of the deceased's cattle and chattels, debts and credits should be made as soon as possible. Two or three neighbours listed and appraised or valued the dead person's 'quick goods' and 'moveable' possessions. Wills and inventories for the townships north of the River Ribble were proved in the courts of the Archdeaconry of Richmond and several are stored in the Lancashire Record Office. Fewer than fifty wills and/or inventories for Alston, Dilworth and Thornley are available for the period 1550–1650. However over 250 exist for the period 1650–1750. After 1750 the proportion of inventories accompanying wills falls considerably.

Although one cannot assume that the inventories were entirely accurate, as the appraisers did vary in their thoroughness, they do provide a valuable source of information concerning the household possessions, livestock holdings, crops and husbandry gear of the late seventeenth- and early eighteenth-century farmer. Obviously the value of the inventories as an economic guide has limitations. Inventories were not usually made for the poor, therefore no matter how meagre the lists were, they reflect the possessions of the better-off.

In most cases the house contents can be described as utilitarian and in some cases sparse. Many of the farms would be of very small acreage and today would be considered small-holdings. Understandably the principal requirements seem to have been something on which to sit, something on which to sleep, something with which to cook and something from which to eat. When one considers the spartan conditions in the farmhouses, one shudders to think how the poor people lived.

Generally speaking, at ground-floor level the houses consisted of the 'kitching', the 'house' (general living room), the 'buttery' (storage), and the 'parlour' (usually a downstairs bedroom). Upstairs the rooms were often named with reference to what was beneath them – thus 'the kitching chamber', 'the buttery chamber', 'the parlour chamber'. The principal bedroom was 'the great chamber' and was often over 'the house'.

John Norcross of Dilworth died in 1705. He was one of the wealthier farmers of the area. In preparing his inventory the appraisers were most meticulous. They moved from room to room, and shed to barn, noting over 200 items

In his kitchen could be found the main fire for cooking purposes. This room was sometimes referred to as the 'fire house'. A pivoted iron frame called a 'rackontree' or 'rackoncrook' enabled iron vessels to be swung over the fire, their height being controlled by a vertical ratchet (a type of contrivance still in use in many houses well into this century). By the fireside were 'fire iorns, crow and tongs', and close by 'one large and one littell brass pot, one littell ould pan, one deep pan, one brod pan and littell one with it, a Chafing dish and Cockell pan [two types of vessel for heating water over the fire], and trenchers [wooden plates]'. Also there was a table and 'one littell Tresst [trestle table]'.

In the 'House' were '6 chayers, 8 quishons [cushions – chairs were not upholstered], 6 stools [in general use around the table for all except the head of the household], a cubord, and a littell chist [storage box]'. Cooking also took place here, as there were 'fire iorn, rackentree, shovell & tonges, frying pan, dripping pan, chafing dish, 4 littell ladells, 3 spits [for roasting meat], striking knife, choping knife, schreading knife, pothooks, smoothing iron, warming pan and candlestick'.

The 'Buttery' contained '88 lbs of Beuther [butter], Backon [bacon], cheesfats [for moulding cheeses], and one salt pye [possibly a salt block], one littell table, bassons [basins], brass spoons, earthenware vessels, potmetell vessels [alloy of lead and copper], and a candlestick'.

The 'Parlor' was used as a bedroom and contained 'Bedstocks and Hanging [probably a four-poster], one feather bed, boulster, one payer of sheets, 2 coverlets, 2 blankets, one ould counter[pane], one chayer and 3 quishons'.

This house had a further storage room referred to as the 'oyel house' (Could this be 'ale house'?). It contained a variety of equipment for making butter, cheese and ale: 'one chayern [churn], one butter tub, 2 cheesepress, one brewing stand, one mash crop and gelker [probably for crushing barley or malt], one stone trough and skip, 8 barralls, 4 gallons [possibly of ale, but more likely to be measures], 3 pigons [wooden pails], 2 flaskets [shallow baskets], 2 forms, a shelf, a table, 2 weyboks [scales] and lead weights, and meall and malt in 3 Arkes [storage chests]'.

Upstairs 'Ye Great Chamber' contained 'one feather bed, 3 boulsters, 2 pillows, an ould bed, one table, 2 littell tables, 2 chayers, 4 quishons, 2 seeled stools [decorated or panelled], a form and white mettell [vessels]'. Clearly this was quite a large room and worthy of a wealthy farmer.

The 'Buttery Chamber' contained 'two payer of bedstocks and hangings, two feather bed boulsters, bed cloaths, one payer of sheets, one blanket, 2 coverlets, 2 pillows, 1 chayer, 2 quishons and one ould chist [probably for storing clothes as wardrobes were not then in use]'. Another room was called 'The Linnon Chamber' and was principally used for storage. It contained 'one table, 13 napkins, 5 payer of fine canvas sheets – one payer marked with an "M", 4 table cloaths, 3 pillow cases and one towell'. A further room, probably small, contained 'one payer of bedstocks, chafe [chaff] bed and bed cloaths on it and one chist'. It should be noticed that all the other beds contained feathers. This would not be an important bedroom and might have been occupied by servants. Most of the farmhouses had at least one chaff bed, some had several. James Bleasdale of Alston (d. 1667) had one feather bed and four chaff beds.

There was obviously a lot of people living in this house. There were eight beds, several of which would be double beds, and six chairs and eight stools in the main living room. It must be remembered that, as well as the family, the farm labourers and servants also often lived at the house. Many farmhouses had 'truckle beds' which could be erected quickly if visitors arrived.

The Norcross house was well equipped with both furniture and cooking equipment to cater for a large household. Nevertheless other local farmers did have one or two luxuries which are not recorded in the Norcross house. Edmund Eccles of Thornley (d. 1703) had 'a clock'. John Bradley of Thornley (d. 1729) had 'a case clock' valued at £2 (about half the value of a good cow). Edward Roades of Thornley (d. 1706) had a 'greet bible', 'won book of amaras works' and 'won little book in ye nook'. He also had a 'seen glasse'. James Norcross of Alston (d. 1715) had 'an old clock' which makes one wonder how long this had been in the family. William Norcross of Alston (d. 1726) had books, a warming pan, a seeing glass and a virginals frame. Thomas Halsall of Alston (d. 1682) had a 'Carpett' in 'ye best Chamber'.

The appraisers of James Norcross noted the farming side of the establishment in equal detail. The livestock was listed as follows: 'one red calving hefer, one red cow and calfe, one red calving cow, one red barren cow, one black calving heffer, one payer of oxen, one payer of 3 year ould bullocks, one payer of twinter [two winter] stears, 3 why [female] calves, one ox calve, one coult, one white horse, one bay horse, and one swine'.

It is worthy of note that the farm carried a very small number of cattle compared with today's large dairy herds. Three hundred years ago there was no advantage to be gained from a large herd. Milk could not be transported satisfactorily in any quantity over even short distances. Preston, which at that time had a small population, would receive its milk from cattle in the immediate vicinity. However, dairy products such as butter and cheese could be taken to the town on horseback, as is reported by Peter Walkden of Chipping in his diary for 1720–30. Most inventories list butter- and cheese-making equipment and some give the amount actually in the house. Lawrence Cottam of Dilworth (d. 1718) had 'twelve hundred weight of cheese' valued at £11 12s. 0d. or 2d. a pound. James Norcross, above, had 88 lbs of butter valued at £2 8s. 8d., or 6½d. per pound.

In husbandry gear James Norcross had a 'cole cart [coal was brought in pannier bags or carts from as far away as Eccleshill, near Blackburn], turf cart [turf was dug from the fell, and was probably in greater use than coal], marell [marl] cart, muck cart & rayths [rakes], hay cart, and spare wheels and axles, 3 sleds [carts on runners were still in general use as wheels were expensive], 4 harrows, 3 plows, 2 ox yoaks' and many items of harness for the horses, for example, '2 pack sadells, traces, neck coller, halters, holms and wantayes'. It is interesting that the term 'wain' or 'wayne' used to describe a farm cart occurs several times in the inventories before 1680, but never afterwards.

As farms had to be largely self-supporting there was quite a lot of arable land in the area, particularly in parts of Thornley which had a lighter soil due to the underlying limestone. Alston soils, apart from a small area of alluvium on the flood plain of the River Ribble, were heavy in some parts and badly drained in others. Dilworth soils were similarly heavy or badly drained. Despite these shortcomings arable crops were grown. Most of the farmers grew barley, wheat or oats. Oxen were the draught animals of the period. Horses were mainly used for riding or for carrying packs or panniers.

There are many other items of interest recorded at other houses. Many of the houses had a 'dishboard'. This would lean against the wall and store crockery in much the same way as a Welsh dresser. Practically all the inventories refer to pewter vessels. Drinking vessels would be almost exclusively made of this metal. It was usually valued by weight at between 7d. and 1s. per pound. William Hothersal of Alston (d. 1679) had 60 lbs of pewter, but 10–40 lbs was more common. Another item often valued by weight was the feather bed. Robert Barker of Birks in Thornley (d. 1663) had one feather bed of '3 stone & 6 lbs weight' and another 'wantinge 2 lbs of 3 stone' whilst he had a boulster of 14 lbs weight. One would certainly be able to sink comfortably into these but, along with sheets and blankets, they would be very necessary in cold damp houses during the winter months.

Smoking was indulged in by at least one farmer, as Henry Shirburne of Thornley (d. 1691) had 'one tobacco boxe of Lignum vitae with all other nesesaryes'.

There are many refences to smoothing irons, which were heated in front of the fire. One refers to 'heaters' also, which suggests the type of hollow smoothing iron into which were inserted shaped pieces of iron which had been heated in the fire.

Most of the houses had a selection of chists and arks. The chists or chests were wooden boxes in which were stored clothing and other possessions. Many were described as 'seeled chists', meaning that they had a carved decoration or were decoratively panelled. The arks were plain wooden boxes used to store meal or malt (for the making of ale) and appeared in various parts of the establishment depending on their contents. Makers of arks were called arkwrights.

References to materials or equipment for the spinning and weaving of wool are not as frequent as one might expect; neither is the existence of many sheep. James Hackinge of Alston (d. 1671) had 'reeles distafes with tow cards & the heckle'. Edward Rhoads of Dilworth (d. 1706) had 'one wool wheel and a pare of cards'. Heckles or hackles and cards were used together for combing out the fibres of the wool prior to spinning. Three inventories refer to looms.

Eight inventories record guns or 'birding pieces', whilst Richard Alston of Thornley (d. 1660) was prepared for all eventualities with 'one birdding peese and a swarde and a hand bow'. As would be expected candlesticks were much in evidence along with 'lanthornes'. These were lanterns having horn rather than glass panes.

As far as Longridge folk three hundred years ago were concerned banks did not exist. If someone wished to borrow money, he or she searched out someone with a surplus. Those with a surplus were keen to lend money, with interest of course, in order to increase their capital. Of the 223 local inventories 100 make reference to money owed to the deceased, whilst only thirteen refer to money owed by the deceased. The latter is hardly surprising, as most of the deceased would be older farmers who no longer had need to borrow.

A detailed analysis of the financial state of those leaving inventories suggests very strongly that there was meagre prosperity among the farming community during the second half of the seventeenth century, but this was followed by a growth in wealth during the first half of the eighteenth century.

This led to widespread replacement of old farmhouses or their modernisation during the second half of the century. This, along with the expansion of the stone industry and cotton handloom weaving, provided further employment for the local people and enabled many of the houses on Fell Brow, Market Place, King Street and Higher Road to be built.

The terms of the wills point to practices current at the time. It was usual on the death of the male farmer for the agricultural side of the property and the house, to pass to the son or sons. However, provision was always made for the widow, who was granted specified accommodation in the house. Thus Robert Hothersall of Alston (d. 1781) wills that '. . . I give . . . the use and occupation of the Lodging Room in the new end of the said messuage above stairs unto my beloved wife Jane . . . And I give . . . to my wife the feather bed and fire iron now being in the said lodging room in the new end.' This points to there being a fireplace in the bedroom, and, significantly, that a recent extension of the house had been made.

Any financial arrangements made for widows usually terminated on re-marriage. Edward Hothersall of Alston (d. 1766) states:

> I give to my beloved wife Catherine five pounds a year duering her natterall life if she lives in my tenement and it is in my mind that it shall be paid to her every quarter or as her need may require . . . and I give her one bed at her owne choice and all thereto belonging . . . but if she marries again and doth not continue my widow then the said five pounds a year shall no longer become due and payable but cease.

Roger Lund of Alston (d. 1730) was quite blunt: 'If my wife do marry the executors pay her £5 and that she clear out from any more title claime'. James Seed of Thornley (d. 1654) was careful to see to the comfort and warmth of his two sisters who lived with him for he arranged, 'my sisters to have a chamber in the west end of the house during their lives and five pounds every year and six wain loads of good terrfe'. James Hackinge of Alston (d. 1671) seems to have anticipated trouble when he inserted in his will, 'if odds or differences between my sayd wife and children the disagreements to be decided by my beloved brother, Adam Rabye that there may be peace and unity again'.

It was not unusual in those days, as now, for money to be willed to the poor. However there were occasions when the deceased wished to be charitable and at the same time boost the number at his funeral. Thus Richard Cottam of Dilworth (d. 1731) wrote: 'one penny and half a cake of bread and a shive of cheese to every poor person as a dole at my ffunerall but if any of the above are not content they shall have nothing'. There were those also whose charitable thoughts were of a more lasting nature. Such was Frances Roades of Dilworth (d. 1696) who left money to 'poore distressed housekeepers of Dilworth'. This was the origin of the Frances Roades Charity which is still in existence today.

William, one of Robert Pye's sons, was probably quite young when his father died in 1663 for his father willed, 'to my sonne William Pye £3 the use thereof yearly untill he bee a good husband and then the £3 shall be bestowed upon a cow to be sett forth for his good and profit'.

Some wills tell a pathetically sad story. Ellen Dobson, spinster of Alston (d. 1690), appears to have been living at Leeds as she has there, according to her inventory, 'one fether bed boulster caddow & blankets' as well as 'one bond with Condition for ye payment of eight pounds at Leeds in ye truncke'. Circumstances then arose which made her return to Alston. These are made clear in the will:

> . . . upon the fourth day of November instant Ellin Dobson of Alston in ye county of Lancaster spinster in the now dwelling house of Thomas Norcross in Alston aforesaid haveing been theare ressidend about two munths beinge with child and near her time of trouble did make and declare her last will according to these words following being of sound mind and memory. I give

unto my sister Ann Hoolle wiffe of John Hoolle of Elsweeck all my goods
and chattells . . .

Most beneficiaries of local wills were the deceased's immediate family or
relatives. However there are wider implications surrounding two recipients.
George Hothersall, innkeeper of Alston (probably of the White Bull), who
died in 1715, left two shillings and sixpence to a 'Mr Vaversor'. George
Hothersall, yeoman of Alston (d. 1720), left ten shillings to 'Sir Walter
Vavasor'. Tom Smith in his *History of Longridge* writes that the Hothersalls
were staunch Catholics and had suffered much for the faith. Sir Walter
Vavasour, a Jesuit priest, was a great friend of the Hothersalls and at that
time was residing in Alston. Mass had to be said secretly and probably took
place frequently at the chapel at Hothersall Hall, as well as in other houses
in the township. Mr Vavasour, another prominent Jesuit, was Sir Walter's
brother. It is reported that he and others were seen in Preston with cockades
in their hats and wearing swords. In 1715 this would be seen as most
provocative. George Green, the high constable of the Hundred of Amounderness, advised the commissioners that 'Mr Vavisor, who is a reputed
priest, is harboured in our town [Alston-cum-Hothersall].[1]

Whilst the two Vavasours survived the 1715 Jacobite rising two other local
men did not. The Ribchester parish register records that John Winckley and
Thomas Shuttleworth, both of Alston, were executed for treason in 1716.

CHAPTER 4

Local Government before 1900

The Alston Book[1]

EACH township was expected to assemble twelve to fourteen of its inhabitants to form a vestry to administer local affairs. In Alston and Dilworth these groups were known as select vestries, that for Dilworth meeting at the Dilworth White Bull, and that for Alston at the Alston White Bull. Fortunately, some of the vestry records for Alston have survived and are contained in a worn, much-handled, leather-bound volume called the Alston Book, which is now kept in the Lancashire Record Office.

Inside the front cover is written:

Alston Book
for Regulating the officers in ye town as they shall fall
in their Course yearly
R.B.

Thus commences a book which is filled with fascinating glimpses into the running of Alston township during the eighteenth century.

The Alston Vestry seems to have been made up entirely from the farmers of the area and contained such names as Hothersall, Grimaldeston, Norcross, Lund, Eccles, Walmsley, Blanchard.

Each year the vestry appointed certain officials to carry out unpaid public duties: overseer of the poor, churchwarden, overseer of the highways and constable. Strictly speaking, members of the vestry had to undertake to hold these offices from time to time. This many of them did, but it was possible to opt out by getting someone else to do the job, and the volunteer was paid to act as substitute. This can be seen clearly in the case of George Ratcliffe, who served on behalf of several people. In fact over the years this man acted as overseer of the poor, constable and churchwarden and on occasions performed the duties of two of these officials in the same year.

Each official was responsible for collecting money (referred to as 'books') from those in the community who were adjudged able to pay. Today we pay one lump sum, but in those days each official collected his own portion. The Alston Book contains the financial accounts of the various officials during part of the eighteenth century. In 1758 George Ratcliffe was overseer of the poor. He paid the house rent of Robert Walton, John Troop, George Abbot, John Travene and William Rigby; he additionally paid Robert Walton for looking after his mother and then paid 4s. 9½d. 'for Death of his mother'; he paid for coal for Richard Bilsborough and the charges made for binding John Travene's son apprentice; he provided 11d. to buy a pair of clogs for John Lund's child; and he also made a contribution to Brindle Poor House, for it was there that some of Alston's poor were accommodated.

Despite the efforts of the overseer, provision for the poor was very limited and many inhabitants remained in great distress. This situation was recognised by several individuals who left wills which attempted to alleviate some of the suffering experienced by the many paupers. It was in this way that many of the local charities originated. It is recorded that:[2]

> Richard Houghton, by indenture of feoffment, dated 14 November, 1613, conveyed to Thomas Whittingham of Whittingham, and three others, one of Over Brockholes, one of Dilworth, and one of Haighton, and their heirs, a close called Wood Crook, in Whittingham, containing by estimation, five acres, upon the trusts declared in a schedule thereto annexed, viz.; to apply the yearly sum of £3 to the poor people of the townships hereafter mentioned, that is to say; the yearly sum of £1 10s. on every St Thomas's day, at the Cross near Longridge Chapel, in Alston; the sum of 15s. on every Good Friday, at the Font-stone within the parish church of Preston; and the sum of 15s. on All Saints day, at the church or chapel of Samlesbury.

The cross is said to be near, not at, the Longridge chapel. Could the cross be the one which once stood in the cross base which is now in the field at the corner of Pinfold Lane?

> Frances Roades, by her will, bearing date 1 February, 1696, and proved in the Archdeaconry Court of Richmond; reciting, that she was possessed of a certain parcel of land, whereon she then lived, desired that her father-in-law, George Singleton, should have the house wherein she then lived, for his life; and all the rest, residue and remainder thereof, with the house, after his death, she appointed to be given to poor distressed house-keepers of Dilworth, for all eternity.

The property referred to is Charity Farm, near Knowle Green.

These two charities are still functioning and monies from them are distributed annually – the Houghton Charity by the Anglican church (but not at the cross), and the Rhodes (or Roades) Charity by the town council.

In addition to the above charities there were several others:[3] Thomas Houghton's (of Woodplumpton) of 1649 which was applied to the poor of Preston, Grimsargh, Broughton, Woodplumpton, Eaves, Catforth, Bartle, Elston and Alston; the Gregson Charity of 1742 and Eccles' of 1777 were combined for the poor of Alston; Jenkinson' Charity of 1777 was again for the poor of Alston as was Berry's Charity of 1803; Henry Townley's Charity of 1776 benefited the poor of Dilworth, but eventually, in the early years of the nineteenth century, the capital was used for the building of a workhouse for the townships of Ribchester, Dutton, Dilworth and Hothersall. Dilworth contributed £325 for this project. The interest formerly used by the charity was henceforward met from the poor rate.

It must be remembered that in the eighteenth century the office of churchwarden was really a civil post, as looking after the church or chapel was the responsibility of every member of the community regardless of religious affiliation. In 1773 we find that George Ratcliffe was church-warden on behalf of the occupant of Alston Hall.[4] In that year he recorded that £2 3s. 5d. was paid for 'wood & carting & workmanship for repairing the Chapel seats and Nales', 1s. was paid for 'washing surpells', while Henry Clarkson received 8d. for half a hundred bricks for the school. Thomas Hacking was also paid for providing straw. This would have been spread on the floor of the chapel and changed from time to time. George Ratcliffe was chapelwarden again in 1784 when the chapel was repaired and enlarged.

In 1777 William Clough was overseer of the highways. It was his respon-sibility to see that roads in Alston were kept in reasonable repair and so he records that he paid for 513 loads of gravel at 2d. per load. Presumably a load was the amount that was put in a cart that would be drawn by a horse. The vestry did not employ a regular workforce. Labourers were hired when required and were paid at the rate of 12d. per day. The accounts suggest that twenty-eight man-days were used to spread the gravel: Richard Hayhurst worked eight days, Thomas Pope and Christopher Corbrick three days each, Henry Cottam five days and William Clough nine days. Perhaps the overseer worked with the men to see that the repairs were carried out satisfactorily. Thomas Carter was employed for one day to repair a plat (bridge). He had one man to help him. William Lund was paid 1s. 4d. for mending hammers and picks.

Gravel was also bought to spread at the gates of the 'Pinfould', which was a small enclosure that was used to pen stray animals, as they were able to wander more freely at that time. The person employed to look after the pinfold was called 'a pinder', hence the use of this term as a surname. The Alston pinfold was near to the entrance to the present Pinfold Lane.

In 1778 George Radcliffe (or Ratcliffe) acted as constable on behalf of Thomas Suddel. He helped with the assessment of land and window tax and went to Preston to hand money to one of the justices. He drew up a list of those eligible for the militia and went to Preston when they were sworn in. On this occasion he spent 9d. with the sergeant. This was an expense he was able to claim and was probably for providing refreshment for himself and maybe the sergeant. He also purchased handcuffs for 2s. 6d. In 1791 the constable, William Lund, paid 2s. 5d. to have the stocks repaired. These were situated at one corner of the churchyard.

It was the duty of the constable to make a report to the justices at the quarter sessions on the condition of roads and the legal requirements of alehouses.

Thus in 1651 James Bleasdale made his report as follows:[5]

> The Constables in Alston in Hothersall doe certifie that the Highway belonginge to Alston Hall formerlie presented is sufficientlie repaired and all the highwayes within the Townshippe are in good repaire the Alehouses Licensed watch and ward duely observed and nothinge p[re]sentable within the Townshipp.

At that time complaints were 'presented' to the sessions and so the expression, 'nothing presentable' means that there were no complaints and that everything was satisfactory.

Although George Radcliffe appears to have been quite willing to act as constable, there were several who, for one reason or another, expressed considerable dislike for the office. In 1649 Richard Greystocke of Hothersall desired to be discharged from constableship. Perhaps he was finding the work onerous, for the justices asked for four men to join the constable in assessments. The following year Thomas Walton asked for assistance to carry out his duties. It must be remembered that the constable, like the other officials, was elected for a term of one year and would have to maintain his own private avocation at the same time. This system did have a serious drawback as there was little continuity from year to year.

There is a well known saying, 'A policeman's lot is not a happy one', and there is, perhaps, no better example of this than the remarkable case of Richard Parkinson. On 12 April 1716 he petitioned the quarter sessions at Preston, saying that he:[6]

> being late Constable of the Townshipp of Alston cum Hothersall on or about the Ninth day of Aprill in the year one thousand seven hundred & fifteen a Warrant was sent to yor Petitioner to apprehend and take the body of Elizabeth Goodshaw of Alston upon suspicion of felony upon which Warrant yor Petitioner took ye sd Elizabeth Goodshaw and brought her before Henry Sowerby of Dutton Esq then Justice of the Peace who ordered yor Petitioner to bring her ye sd Elizabeth Goodshaw to her father William Goodshaw of Alston af[ore]sd to keep her till one Jane Daniell one of her Confederates should be taken and to charge the sd William Goodshaw to keep her safe. But so it happened may it please yor Wor[shi]pps that the sd Elizabeth Goodshaw made her escape sometime after she was taken Upon which escape yor Petitioner was bound over to appear at the last Summer assizes and was there prosecuted upon the sd escape to free himself of which prosecution it cost yor Petitioner the sume of six pounds three shillings and four pence which sd sume some of the Chief Inhabitants of ye Townshipp of Alston did mutually agree should be repaid to yor Petitioner by an assessment to be laid through the sd Townshipp but others of them refused the same so that yor Petitioner is still out of pocket the af[ore]sd sume of six pounds three shillings & fourpence Wherefore the premises considered Yor Petitioner humbly begs yor Worshipps releif and assistance in this his extraordinary case and Yor Petitioner will ever pray etc.

[signed] Richard Parkinson
Recommended to the town [Justices' decision]

Justice was done, as the constable was reimbursed by a levy on the townspeople. It should be noted, however, that the cost imposed on the constable was quite considerable. If comparisons are made this will be seen more clearly. At 12d. per day a workman would have to labour for 123 days, or a farmer would have to sell two cows, in order to meet the costs. No wonder Richard Parkinson was acutely disturbed.

Although the major part of the Alston Book is made up of accounts, there are a few entries which give added interest to the reader. Corruption, manipulation and exploitation of local councils is not new. Even Alston seems to have been confronted by such problems. It has been noted that George Radcliffe performed official duties so frequently that he obviously knew what was going on in the township. Who better, therefore, to spot an attempt by Edward Blanchard to have the road to his farm repaired at the town's expense in 1761 when it had been decided otherwise, thirty-eight years earlier, at a meeting in 1723. Now Blanchard could possibly have pleaded ignorance of such an old rule had he not attempted to remove the offending minute from the book. Unfortunately for him his actions were observed by Ratcliffe who decided that the crime was worthy of a full-page report in the book.

The background to the case was that in 1723 John Parkinson of Horn Plat (in Alston Lane) who was overseer of the highways, had repaired the bridge (platt) at Horn Plat and then charged the cost, 4s., to the highways account. Radcliffe reported that:[7]

> At that time the Townsmen had not alow the Acctt nor suffer the same to pass at the Town's Charge At any rate after he got the Town's Men to meet 3 or 4 sepperate times but at last it was agreed By the Town's Men to alow the above sd charge for that time and then to enter into an agreement never to repair any more in that Lean [lane] betwixt Wm Salthouse House End And Bought Fould – which agreement was written In this Book and signed by 12 or 14 men at that meeting.

The agreement whereby the township was not liable to repair the road was then written in the Alston Book. However, in 1761, Edward Blanchard 'did go to Wm. Grimbledestons and saw the Book upon a shelf in the house. He sd to Wm wife he wod take the Book and bring it again in a few days'. When Blanchard returned to the White Bull on Court Day:

> he laid the Book in the parlour windw – Geo Charnley takes the Book to look in it and finds half a leaf in it Geo Charnley came and asked me if I remembered there was half a leaf in the Townes Book. I said there was no such thing. I did after the Stuerd of the Court was gone go into the Sd parlor, and when I sat down Edwd. got up and did take the Book out of the sd room

and did go the Mr Hide [the landlord] for a candle and did go up stares with the Book and I saw him take the half leaf out.

Upon investigation it was found that the page which had been torn out was that bearing the agreement of 1723, as well as other items. Radcliffe concluded by stating that, 'this I will sertyfie for truth upon oath if required'.

Changes in Local Government

LOCAL government, as exercised by the select vestry, disappeared in the nineteenth century. Such a system, where the officers worked in an amateur capacity and changed annually, inevitably leading to a lack of continuity and efficiency, was at long last considered unsatisfactory.

The passing of the Poor Law Act in 1834 made redundant the overseer of the poor and passed his work to poor law guardians operating in the wider context of the Preston Union, which stretched from the moors of Bowland to the mosses near Longton. The first election of guardians took place in March 1838. Preston had six guardians while Alston, Dilworth, Hothersall and Dutton had one each. Guardians had to be persons of substance as they had to have property of annual value or rental of at least £20 – quite a sum in those days.

The Act required the appointment of full-time professional relieving officers. For this purpose the rural townships in this area were grouped together as the Alston District where Mr William Halsall was appointed at an annual salary of £60.[8] At that time he was living at No. 8 King Street, but later moved to Chapel Hill.

Soon afterwards the board of guardians advertised for a medical officer:[9]

whose duties . . . will include attendance and supply of medicines, midwifery, vaccination of children and for which a written order from the Relieving Officer or other competent authority shall be given. The District of Alston will include the Workhouse of Ribchester.

Four applicants tendered for the post – two from Preston and two from Longridge. Although the Preston doctors offered lower tenders, the post was offered to Dr Edmund Eccles of Newtown as it was thought desirable to appoint a local person. His salary was £55.

In 1838, the number of recorded paupers in the Alston District was quite considerable – Dutton seventy-three, Alston thirty-four, Ribchester 129, Grimsargh eight, Elston two, Dilworth thirteen, Hothersall none, Ribbleton four: a total of 263. There were sixty-three in the workhouse. This was out of a population of 4,287.[10]

Although the select vestry was finished, that part of its work concerning the church continued. The community was still expected to support and maintain it. A report in July 1854 informed:[11]

On Monday the 10th inst. a meeting was held in the vestry of St Lawrence Church, Longridge, for the purpose of examining the accounts of the churchwardens of the townships of Dilworth and Alston for the past year . . . The next business was the laying of a rate for the repairs of the church, and for defraying the necessary expenses attending divine service. Mr Wm. Halsall, the senior churchwarden, moved, seconded by Mr Parkinson, yeoman, that a rate of one penny in the pound on the above townships be laid . . . Mr Halsall's motion was carried unanimously. Altogether the meeting was marked by cordiality and good feeling.

In March 1881 the annual township meeting for the ratepayers of Alston was held,[12] at which there was much discussion about the state of the roads and footpaths. Mr Waring was obviously conscious of the social status of the occupants of the large houses on Lower Lane when he commented sarcastically that 'He would not say anything about the state of the roads. They all knew their condition as well as he did, but he might just observe that there was a good footpath on the Lower Lane and a very poor one by the Old Oak Inn. This did not matter much, as only the plebeian class had to walk on the latter'. Mr Booth added:

They must take into account that the population of Alston was every year increasing and the highways were therefore subjected to increased traffic, and through the building of the county asylum at Whittingham and other things. Another subject to speak about – the footpaths. Their state was simply disgraceful. It was the system that was at fault – not the surveyor. Their footpaths were made of clay with a scattering of cinders on the top and after a frost especially, the clay was turned into a spongy kind of matter, and anyone walking along them had to 'plodge' through the dirt as well as they could. It was high time the ratepayers took this matter in hand and tried to do something. He would propose a committee of ratepayers be appointed to confer with the surveyor with a view to making some pavement improvement, and that the ratepayers of Dilworth be asked to appoint a similar committee to work conjointly.

The reasons for the development of a village at Longridge have been stated earlier, and its peculiar position, lying astride township boundaries, has also been stressed. As an administrative unit Longridge did not exist, but instead was governed as part of either Alston or Dilworth. In the growing village, with its increasing need for good public services, this became a serious problem, and in the 1870s and early 1880s there was pressure for a Longridge authority to be formed. Finally in 1883 Longridge Board of Health was created. This was an amalgamation of the townships of Alston and Dilworth, with its focus at Longridge village. For the first time Long- ridge officially existed! In 1894 the local board became Longridge

Urban District and that authority remained unchanged until local govern-ment reforms in 1974, when the area was included within the new borough of Ribble Valley.

Much of the early work of the local board was concerned with public health.[13] A common feature of nineteenth-century Longridge was the presence of pigs in the village, a great number of the residents having a pig sty attached to or close to their houses. Soon after its formation the board received an order that pig sties should be at least 100 feet from any dwelling. This caused great consternation for most householders would have found it impossible to comply with the order. The board suggested that, as this was a country district, thirty feet was sufficient. This distance proved unaccept-able to higher authorities, who offered fifty feet as an acceptable compro-mise. The board replied that the new ruling would prevent 70–80% of the population from keeping pigs. The result was that the number of pigs in the village was severely reduced.

Household effluent was also a major problem. In 1892 the inspector of nuisances reported that, out of 700 houses in the village, 307 were provided with tanks into which the whole of the privy and other sewage matter emptied. All of which, prior to the board's decision to adopt the tank system, had escaped into brooks and ditches in the neighbourhood. The contents of the tanks were periodically removed and sold to local farmers for tillage puposes. A further 100 houses were provided with covered ash-pits which had the effect of materially lessening the impure liquid getting into local streams.

In 1884 the board decided to erect nameplates on the streets. Once they were in position Mr Woolley, the schoolmaster, pointed out that many were incorrectly spelt, and the offending plates had to be removed and replaced with correct ones. The board also suggested that a footbridge should be erected at the level crossing in Berry Lane, as that spot was particularly dangerous between 5 and 6 p.m. when the mill workers were going home, but this suggestion was never implemented.

CHAPTER 5

Military History

The Civil War

FROM the seventeenth century onwards there are many documents which help us understand better the conditions prevailing as they affected the ordinary inhabitants. Perhaps the best of these sources are the quarter sessions records, where social conditions as well as criminal activities were considered.

One of the most traumatic periods in our history occurred in the middle of the seventeenth century with the civil war which resulted in a sad and lamentable state of affairs in Lancashire. Disease was rife, probably due to malnutrition caused by scarcity of food. The price of grain rose sharply so that the poor could not afford bread and were often forced to beg. In addition, many local families were devastated by deaths resulting directly from military action. Whilst the tactics and strategies associated with the victories and defeats of the armies have long been publicised and analysed, the effects of the war on the local populace has often been overlooked as it did not have a relevance to the overall conduct of the war. The plight of four local women will serve well to illustrate local conditions at the time. Although they are from neighbouring townships, rather than Alston or Dilworth, their circumstances were fairly typical.

During the course of the war the loyalty of the people of Lancashire was divided. Some supported parliament and some the king. It is probable that the ordinary working man was indifferent to either cause, but usually was obliged to follow the allegiance of his employer. Parts of Lancashire became battlegrounds as the strategic position of the county was well recognised. In those days armies on the move did not have organised food supplies, but were expected to feed themselves from the land which they passed through.

In 1644 a section of the king's army was besieged in York. The king's nephew, Prince Rupert, was campaigning in Cheshire when he was ordered to proceed to the relief of York. On his way through Lancashire his renowned and feared cavalry descended on Bolton and wreaked havoc in what became known as the 'Massacre of Bolton'. Rupert's route then took him along the Ribble Valley, where his men looted and plundered as they went. Margaret Salisbury and her husband lived on their route at Chaigley. They had worked hard on the land to maintain themselves and their children, and the effect of Rupert's passage was to blight their lives for years to come. In 1649 Margaret was forced to petition the quarter sessions as follows:[1]

> That yor peticoner for the space of 30 years and upwards hath lived togeather wth her husband throw their owne payne and hard industrye noe what chargable to their neighbours in any sorte But about 5 years agoe yor peticoner and her late husband suffered great losse to their utter undoeing through plunder by Prince Ruperts Armye since which tyme yor peticoners husband dyed leaveing yor peticoner a charge of nyne smale poore children to bring up and her house to take from yeare to yeare And now by reason of this great dearth and scarsitye of Corne yor peticoner and her smale children are likely to be lost for want of food and Releiffe and to be exposed to the misseryes of this wide and woefull world haveing noe house nor habitacon to inhabit in wth her smale children.
>
> May it please yor wo[rshi]pps to take into consideracon your petticoners deplorable condicon And to grant your Warrant to the Overseers for the poore within Aighton, Baley & Chadgley that yor petticoner according to the statute in that case provyded may be releived wth some poore house or place to sitt in and receive some smale exhibicon for their p[re]sent livelyhood . . .

Margaret refers to a dearth and scarcity of corn. J. M. Stratton in *Agricultural Records* records that in 1646 the price of wheat was 48s. per quarter, but by 1648 it had risen to 85s. per quarter because this was 'A most exceeding wet year, neither frost nor snow all the Winter for more than 6 days in all' (Evelyn), followed by 'a prodigiously wet summer, very cold'. In consequence of this wet weather there was a great scarcity of grain and prices went up accordingly. 1649 was little better: although wheat fell to 80s. per quarter the year was recorded as a famine year. Margaret Salisbury and other widows had enough problems without those added by climatic vicissitudes. By 1654 several good harvests and the end of the war resulted in the price of wheat falling to 26s. 8d. per quarter. One can only hope that Margaret and her family survived to enjoy better times.

Thomas Pope of Whittingham was killed fighting for parliament during the siege at Bolton. He left a widow and a young baby and, since they were otherwise destitute, it was to Thomas's father that they turned for help. But in 1647 the widow, Anne Pope, petitioned to the quarter sessions, saying that:[2]

> yor peticoner heretofore int[er]married wth Thomas Pope sonne of Richard Pope of Whittingham in the countie of Lancaster husbandman wth the free consent after much and many intreaties of the said Richard Pope wch said Thomas Pope was a listed soldier under the comand of Lie[uten]ent Collonell Alex[ander] Rigby and was in the parliaments service from the xiiijth day of September 1643 till the Battaile at Boulton where he received such mortall wound that within sixteene days next after hee dyed.

Anne had been left with a daughter only thirty weeks old, and had no estate, but hoped that she could be supported by her father-in-law. It was not to be, however:

> the said Richard Pope after his sonnes death soone wthdrew his sonnes meanes from yor pet[icone]r and now of late hath warned yor peticoner & her little child to bee gone quite out of the house wher they have dwelled at & evr since the death of the said Thomas Pope and to the end that he the said Richard Pope may thence expell yor peticoner & her child hee hath pulled downe the walls both of the fire house & chamber wherein they lodged and hath almost starved yor pet[icone]r & her child & refuseth to give any maintenance to the said child

Anne's plight, and that of the child, were movingly expressed – as was the fear, on the part of the parish authorities, that they would end up paying poor relief:

> the said Richard Pope is grandfather to the said child & for that the said child is destitute of all meanes of livelyhood & in regard that yor peticoner is soe pore that she is not able to relieve it is likely to bee burthensome to the said parrishe unles the said Richard Pope whoe is able & by the lawe ought to maintaine it shalbee by yor worr[shi]pps order compelled soe to doe

It was asked that an order should be made for Richard Pope to maintain the child, and 'suffer it & yor peticoner to continue theire habitacon in the house whereunto it is the next comeinge ten[eme]nt'. Anne's petition received a sympathetic hearing after which the justices recommended that 'the grand-fathers of both syde shall p[ro]porconably maintayne the child & Pope to repair the house againe wthin one month or to find her some place or to bee bound to good behaviour'. No matter how fair this judgement was, Anne's life can hardly have been a happy one with her reluctant father-in-law on her doorstep.

Bridgett Hesketh and her husband, of Aighton, lived contentedly with their three small children until the armies passed through and plundered their goods and crops. This loss combined, in later years, with poor harvests and high prices brought the family to a state of great distress. Sadly Bridgett's husband felt unable to share his family's misfortune and left them. Quite unable to cope, Bridgett had to vacate her house and was left with no alternative but to petition the sessions. The words of Bridgett's petition, in 1649, express most graphically the hopelessness of her situation:[3]

> yor peticoners husband was a man of good creditt and of a competent estate at their intermarriage by whom it pleased the Almightie to blesse yor peticoner wth 3 smale children But yor peticoners said husband (in theis distracted tymes) haveing sufferred great losse in his goods by plunder wth the Armies as also by other disastrous happs soe that yor peticoner her said

husband and poore children were brought to great want & indigencye And yor peticoners sayd husband not willinge to p[ar]take wth his wife & children in want & misserye sith in these dearth yeares the stafe of bread was almost taken from amongst us. About halfe a yeare agoe hath left yor peticoner and poore children harbourles & succourlesse and exposed to woefull misseryes of this ruthles world.

May it please your good wo[rshi]pps to take into consideracon your peticon[ers] deplorable condicon being a degree belowe misserie itselfe haveinge noe other storehouse than the harts of all those whom the Lord wilbe pleased to touch wth a selfe feeleing notion of distressed penurye As to grant yor Warrant to the ov[er]seers of the poore wthin Aighton Baley & Chadgley that yor poore peticon[er] & her smale children may be relieved according to the statute in that case provided and to be alowed some little place to sitt in & any smale exibition for their present livelyhood.

She asked the justices for help from the local community, whereby the overseer would relieve her, but her eloquent petition was not answered in the anticipated way. The verdict of the court was: 'Benjamin Eccles ye grandfather to maintaine'.

Although each township had an overseer of the poor and some funds available for such relief, these were very limited, and wherever possible it was expected, and considered right, that relatives should provide any necessary support.

Elizabeth Hayhurst's soldier husband died in Ireland in 1648. She was left with four children. In recent years she and her family had lived in several local townships – Chipping, Ribbleton, Fulwood and Haighton. Furthermore she had no known relatives on whom to call for support. In January 1649 she was left with no alternative but to place her plight before the justices:[4]

. . . yor pet[iconers] husband about halfe a yeare since listed himself a souldier under the comand of Captaine Potter in the Regiment of Colonell Moore for the service of Ireland who sithence is slayne by the enemy there and hath left behynde him yor pet[iconer] and ffoure smale ffatherles children who are all of them destitute of meanes for theire subsistance and livelyhood but are necessitated to begg for their relieffe

That yor said pet[iconer] and her children have lived for almost foure yeares last past wthin the towneshippe of Haighton but now are destitute of houseroom wherein to inhabite and are necessitated many tymes to lye wthout dores for wante of lodginge.

That John and Anne Hayhurste 2 of yor pet[iconers] oldest children (ye one beinge about 12 yeares old and the other beinge about 11 yeres old) were borne wthin the towne of Chippinge, and that Margaret Hayhurste yor said pet[iconers] third childe (beinge about 9 yeares of age) was borne wthin the townshippe of Ribbleton, and Ellen Hayhurste yor pet[iconers] other daughter beinge about 5 yeares old was borne wthin the towneshippe of ffulwood.

That yor said pet[iconer] and her children have noe frends or kindred wch are (to theire knowledge) by lawe compellable to p[ro]vide for them or any of them.

She requested that the maintenance of the children should be provided by the overseers of the townships where they were born, and that the overseer at Haighton, where the family had lived for four years, should provide a house. In this rather complicated case the justices did not accede to Elizabeth's request, but decided that the overseers of the poor for Broughton should provide for them.

Although no battles were fought at Longridge, it is recorded that in August 1648, Cromwell, with his army, crossed from Yorkshire and spent the night at Stonyhurst. It would appear that his forward cavalry, on reaching Longridge, first spotted their enemy. Captain Hodgson wrote:[5] '. . . and the next morning . . . at Langridge Chapel our horse gleaned up a considerable parcel of the enemy, and fought them all the way until within a mile of Preston'. The Royalists fell back to positions nearer Preston, at Ribbleton Moor, where the main battle was fought. At that time much of the land hereabouts would be unenclosed and therefore suitable for cavalry activity.

An entry in the Ribchester parish register provides perhaps the most remarkable local reference to the conflict. The burials section for 1736 records: 'Jan 16 William Wedker a Cavalier aged 122 de Alston'. This prompted T. Smith to write:[6]

> At the Church of Ribchester was interred, in all probability, the last survivor of all who had borne arms in the war between Charles I and the parliament. William Walker had a horse killed under him at the Battle of Edge Hill (1642); how long he retained his mental faculties I do not know; if nearly to the close of life he must have been a living chronicle, extremely interesting and curious.

Further Military Connections

THE restoration of the monarchy in 1660 was a time when it was felt that questionable activities during the commonwealth period could be exposed and petitions concerning that period looked upon sympathetically. In 1661 the inhabitants of Alston complained to the quarter sessions of the conduct of the constable and assessors during the previous seventeen years. Apparently these offices had been restricted to a selected few who had levied taxes for the quartering of soldiers and the holding of Royalist soldiers, but had never rendered any account to show how the money was spent.[7]

> That ye Constable and assessors for ye sayed township have for ye most part dueringe ye space of 17 yeares last past continued & exercized the offices of Constable & Assessor within the sayed townshipp amongst themselves dueringe which tyme they have used & still doe continue to quarter such

souldiers as comes for quarter or such as have beene seq[uestere]d. for beinge in his late Majesties servis and on others most loyall subjects yt they have & still doe continue to lay taxacons & gather the same without renderinge Any Account for ye same . . .

Your peticoners humbly pray this hon'ble Bench that ye Constable and Assessors for the sayed Townshipp that they may give an Accompt to your peticoners or some of them of such layes & taxacons that have been layed payed & gathered since his Majesties most happie Restoracon And as much longer as this hon'ble Bench shall think fitt And that within a convenient tyme after they may bee injoyned to answer for such money as shall appear to be in theire hands . . .'

The inhabitants were duly rewarded, for the justices ordered the constable and assessors to give an account of their finances.

After the Jacobite rebellion of 1715 small groups of soldiers were stationed throughout the country to search out remaining rebels. In this area there was much support for the Jacobite cause, often including the harbouring of insurgents, and to counter this a group of soldiers was stationed in barracks at the north end of Longridge Fell in Chaigley. Barracks Farm in Chaigley is probably close to the spot. The imposition of martial law and the patrols of the troops would not be popular hereabouts.

When there were extensive troop movements, townships along and close to the route were expected to assist with transport. In 1721 Richard Parkinson, constable, claimed five shillings for expenses incurred when he:[8] 'Sent one carriage five horses wth Collonell Keir's Dragoons from Preston to Garstang one day out, but came wth two carriages to Preston being so lumbered thro' very bad roads'. This also serves to remind us of the parlous state of the highways at that time.

In 1745, at the time of the second Jacobite rebellion, an invasion from Scotland was expected, and to meet this threat a military force was assembled locally and extra contributions were levied on the townships. Alston produced £41 11s. 0d.[9] It has always been the duty of each township to provide soldiers if and when the need arose, and it was the task of the constable to list all eligible men in his township and ensure that they reported whenever required. In 1778 George Radcliffe, constable, claimed two shillings expenses for:[10] 'Numbering the town and making Dublicate for militia. Going to Preston when the militia was sworn in and spent with the sergeant 9d.' It is probable that he went with the sergeant to an inn for refreshment.

The arrival of soldiers has always caused a stir of excitement in a local community, especially a rural one such as Longridge, and this was particularly so in the middle of the nineteenth century. During the Crimean War of 1854–5 a battalion of soldiers made its camp on Jeffrey Hill close to Forty-Acres Farm. Sad to say, their conduct left much to be desired and the community which had welcomed their arrival was glad to see them go. However, Longridge Fell continued to be used as a training ground for the

Soldiers from the 1st Battalion, the Manchester Regiment marching past the Forrests Arms on their way to camp at Chipping after the South African War (the Boer War) in about 1902.

army, who found there a different kind of enemy to force their withdrawal. On the 13 October 1855 the *Preston Pilot* reported:[11]

On Monday morning, a detachment from the depot battalion, consisting of two captains, two subalterns, seven sergeants, and 193 rank and file, marched from Fulwood garrison for the purpose of being encamped on Longridge Fell. The camp equipage had been previously forwarded. While encamped the men will be taught the use of the minie rifle, the ground being well adapted for practising firing at a long distance. Some of the youngsters, we believe, (in heavy marching order) found it difficult to keep up with the detachment, and had to fall out. Captain Cassidy, of the 34th, is in command. The camp is some distance from the village of Longridge. The weather, since Monday, has been rather unfavourable for a commencement under canvas, and doubtless the men will have found it a different thing to being lodged in warm and comfortable barracks. It will be a capital training for the men previous to joining their regiments to which they belong, and which have done such good service in the Crimea.

A month later the paper reported the removal of the camp:[12] 'in consequence of the very unpropitious state of the weather, combined with the bleak and exposed site of the camp, the men received orders to strike their tents, and they returned into barracks here last night'.

The newspaper also recorded the type of incident which led to the unpopularity of the camps.[13] A labourer from Dilworth, named Richard Wilding, was returning, at about 9 p.m. on a Sunday evening, from the military camp where he had been indulging in a few glasses of ale. He was met on the highway by a private in the 97th Regiment, named Richard Allen,

*This beacon on Tootle
Heights was erected in 1902
to commemorate the coronation of Edward VII. A bonfire
here also celebrated the
marriage of the Prince and
Princess of Wales in 1862.*

who demanded his money and, after seizing him by the collar, struck him several times on the head with his belt. Allen threw Wilding down, jumped on him and rifled his pockets, but as he attempted to escape he was captured by patrolling guards from the camp.

Tootle Heights

TOOTLE Heights is perhaps less well known now than it used to be. The name itself is most intriguing, but particularly so when considered along with two of the principal roads nearby, Berry Lane and Kestor Lane. It would be convenient to assume that Berry Lane is named after a person, but in the absence of documentary evidence or oral tradition this is by no means certain. Old maps show the spelling as 'Bury'. Similarly, Kestor Lane is shown on old maps as Caster Lane. The two words 'Bury' and 'Caster' have most interesting philological origins: 'caster' was a word used to describe some type of fortification or stronghold and is frequently used as a suffix in the names of settlements with Roman associations, while 'Bury' originates in an Old English or Anglo-Saxon word which means much the same as 'Caster'. Is it a coincidence that these two roads with names of common derivation should both be heading for a similar spot on the summit of the ridge, bearing in mind the common practice, in the past, of naming roads from the places they were going to or from? Was there indeed some sort of fortification on the ridge in the distant past?

A quarter of a mile from where these two roads meet the fell road is the feature called Tootle Height. The word 'Tootle' has a significant derivation also. It is a variation of Tot or Toot Hill, 'Tot' being an Old English word meaning a look-out place' or an 'eminence with a view'. Were the two roads leading to a fortified look-out post? Unfortunately any evidence of such a post has now probably been quarried away.

There are several variations of the spelling which have been used from time to time, for example: Tootle, Tootal, Toothill with Height or Heights. This name is by no means peculiar to Longridge. It occurs in many parts of England and Wales, and was often used when designating a site of greater altitude than its neighbours, with a clear view of the surrounding area. There is no doubt that the site would be a most suitable one for viewing the distant landscape or conversely a point which would be visible from afar. This attribute would account for its use as a site for a beacon in the seventeenth century. A quarter sessions document of 1690 refers to the 'Repair of Longridge Beacon'. In 1690 the High Constable of the Hundred of Blackburn organised 'the repairing & making ready of Longridge Beacon'. He then submitted the bill to the quarter sessions at Preston for approval and payment:[14]

	£ s d
for pitch, tar & rundlet as appears by mr Nowells note	00 15 04
for carriage betwixt Longrige & Preston & expences	00 03 –
Pd for wood to John Hackin carpenter	00 06 –
for a fleyk to be screen to ye watchmen	00 01 –
for workmanshipp	00 04 –
for an iron plate to set the barrell of pitch on	00 01 6
	01 10 10

ffor watchmen there is twelvepence a man for the day & night to be added since they was set to watch there, begininge on Tuesday the 15th day of this instant July.

[A rundlet was a small barrel, and a fleyk was a wicker screen.]

The sudden repair and manning of the beacon day and night was probably caused by the troubles in Ireland. James II was deposed in 1688 and replaced by William of Orange. By 1690 James was in Dublin gathering together an army of Jacobites. William crossed to Ireland to meet this threat, but was worried that his absence would encourage the French fleet to land an invasion force in England in support of the Jacobites. Beacons were therefore prepared so that an invasion could be signalled across the land by lighting them. In the event, William won the Battle of the Boyne on 1 July, and the French fleet was defeated in the Channel. The document suggests that the beacon had been in position prior to this emergency, but had fallen into disrepair, and this is almost certainly the case, as Lord Burgley's map of 1590 shows a beacon at Longridge. A short time prior to that date it might have been used to warn of the approach of the Spanish Armada.

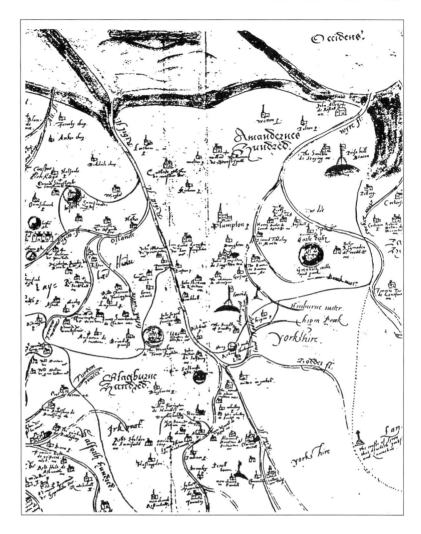

Part of Lord Burghley's map of 1590. The beacon at Longridge (Lonrid) is in the centre of this part of the map. The beacon is shown as a small rundlet (barrel) for pitch on top of a frame. The orientation of this map can be confusing as west (Occidens) is at the top.

The Heights have long been recognised as a significant prominence in the area. A flag was flown there on the proclamation of peace after the Crimean War in 1856. Six years later, in 1862, the marriage of the Prince and Princess of Wales was marked by the burning of a huge bonfire on this spot. Again a beacon or bonfire was erected on Tootle Heights in 1902 to celebrate the coronation of Edward VII.

CHAPTER 6

Quarries and Reservoirs

THE value of the gritstone of the Longridge area for house and farm building had long been recognised. Small delphs were opened in many places prior to the nineteenth century when stone was required for specific local projects. The early years of the nineteenth century saw the rapid development of the cotton industry in the Lancashire towns, and large amounts of stone were required for the mills, the houses, new churches, the new imposing town halls and the docks which handled the incoming raw materials and the export of the manufactured goods. Longridge stone was then required in gradually increasing quantities. Tootle Heights was seen as a source of vast amounts of this commodity and so the ridge was invaded by an ever-increasing army of quarrymen hacking away at the rock under the supervision of the local quarrymasters. Thus were formed Copy, Nook Fold, Spencer's, Fleming's, Broomhill, West End and New England quarries. The results of their labours can be seen in Berry Lane and the local churches, as well as further afield in, for example, Preston – the parish church, St Walburge's Church (though not its spire), Fishergate Baptist Church, St Mark's Church, Fulwood Barracks, Harris Museum and Library, Preston Railway Station – as well as Bolton Parish Church, the Promenade at Blackpool, Blackpool Town Hall, Liverpool Docks and Fleetwood Docks, to mention but a few.

The 1871 census records that there were 182 men from Longridge employed in the stone industry either in the quarries or as stone masons, which was about 25% of the total male workforce of the village. There must have been about as many again from outside the village, as Tom Smith quotes a figure of 400 men employed in the mid-1870s. Many certainly arrived each day by train. By 1881 there had been a slight fall to 164 village men employed with stone, and after this date the fortunes of the trade slumped more rapidly. Smith writes thus:[1]'The causes of the bad trade seem to be the keen competition from Yorkshire and Wales, and the prohibitory rates charged by the Railway Co. for carriage. In this matter, and other things, the owners of the Preston and Longridge Railway have displayed a poor conception of their duties as a carrying company. Of course there is no competition, and, like Corporations, Railway Companies have proverbially no conscience'. There were other reasons also, such as a deterioration in the

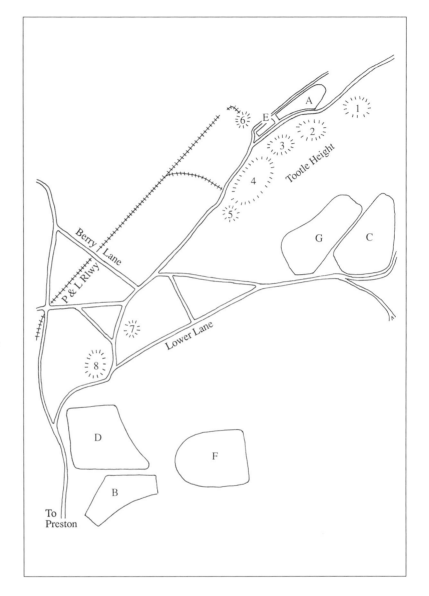

Longridge quarries and
reservoirs.

Quarries:
1–5 The Tootle Height
      complex of quarries.
1   Copy Quarry
2   Nook Fold Quarry
3   Spencer's Quarry
4   Fleming's, Railway,
      Croft's, West End, New
      England Quarries
5   Broom Hill Quarry
6   Lord's Quarry (on
      Derby land)
7   Old Quarry
8   Chapel Hill Quarries

Reservoirs:
A   Dilworth Upper
B   Alston No. 3
C   Spade Mill No. 1
D   Alston No. 2
E   Dilworth Lower
F   Alston No. 1
G   Spade Mill No. 2

quality of some of the stone beds and, above all, greater use of brick and,
later, concrete. Although the larger concerns pulled out, stone extraction by
small firms continued on an ever-diminishing scale for a number of years,
but even this eventually ceased. All the quarries are long since closed, but
Copy Quarry was re-opened briefly to provide hardcore for the M55
motorway to Blackpool, and afterwards was landscaped. A pile of rubble
still marks the site of Green Bank farmhouse.

Inevitably there is an element of danger in quarrying and accidents
did occur at Longridge, but mercifully they were few in number. Several

Tootle Heights Park in the early 1900s.

were reported in the *Preston Pilot*. The following, in September 1838, is an example:[2]

> John Norcross, about 30 years of age, was in the act of wheeling a barrow over a plank on the rock of Mr Spencer's quarry at Longridge when he unfortunately stepped off the plank and was precipitated to the bottom of the rock, some 30 yards. He was dreadfully bruised about the head. Mr Eccles, surgeon, was promptly on the spot, but all efforts to assist him were in vain. He lingered till one o'clock when death put a period to his sufferings. An inquest before John Hargreaves and a respectable jury gave a verdict of accidental death.

The storing of explosives at quarries is quite a problem. Not only do they have to be kept secure, but they must also be kept dry. At one quarry, in 1850, a dry spot was certainly found, but with disastrous consequences, as the *Preston Pilot* reported:[3]

> On Saturday last an explosion of gunpowder took place at Mr Parson's quarry, Longridge, which was fortunately attended with less mischief than might have been anticipated from such an accident. It appears that two barrels of gunpowder, intended for blasting purposes, were deposited in the smithy, (a most unlikely place, we should say, to use for any such purpose, though that is the place where it has always been kept) when a spark communicated with one of the barrels, and they both exploded with a most fearful report, carrying away the roof of the building, and scattering the various things contiguous, in every direction. One of the workmen was very much burnt, but we are glad to say that he is now recovering. His escape from being blown to atoms is most wonderful.

Broad Walk, Tootle Heights Park in the early 1900s.

Band concert on Tootle Heights Park in the early 1900s.

However, some of the quarry masters were keen to try out new ideas in order to improve efficiency, as can be seen from this report in March 1856:[4]

· Some interesting experiments were made at Messrs Cooper and Tullis's quarry at Longridge on Tuesday afternoon. The galvanic battery was made use of for the purpose, but being a first attempt the blast was not so complete as a little practice will no doubt make it. The object sought to be attained is the removal of immense masses of stone by one operation.

Recruiting meeting, 20 May 1915. The amphitheatre of the Tootle Heights Park was the setting for this large gathering of village folk. The union flag fluttered in the breeze as speakers encouraged the young men to join the army.

Safety precautions in the nineteenth century were not as stringent as they are now, but it still comes as a surprise to find that Chapel Hill Quarry was not fenced, even though the field into which the workings were eating was in regular use. In 1857, William Dickinson, who was a shoemaker, lodged in Newtown with Mr & Mrs Wilson. After a night out at the end of May he met his death whilst carrying out a request for his landlady:[5]

On Tuesday, Mr Myres held an inquest at the Duke William public-house, in Longridge, on view of the body of Wm. Dickinson, aged 47 years. It appeared that about twelve o'clock on Sunday night, the deceased was requested by Mrs Wilson, wife of John Wilson, at whose house he lodged, to go into a field adjoining the house to look after a cow about to calve. The deceased was not quite sober at the time. About twenty minutes afterwards, as Dickinson did not return to the house, Mr Wilson went into the field to look for him, and after searching for a short time he discovered Dickinson lying in the bottom of a stone quarry that was parallel with one side of the field. He was lying on his back, and was bleeding profusely from a large wound at the back of his head. He was lying four or five yards from the breast of the rock. He was conveyed to the residence of Mr Wilson, but died in about ten minutes after reaching there. The rock above where he was found is stepped, it is not quite perpendicular. The field above the quarry is not in any manner protected, so that a person unaccustomed to the field might, on a dark night, walk over the field into the quarry. The quarry is about eighteen yards deep. There is no road through the field, but it is a dangerous place both for cattle and persons in the dark.

The jury returned a verdict of 'Accidental death' coupling the verdict with the expression of their opinion that the field above the quarry in which the deceased was killed ought to be fenced off by the owner, so to prevent the recurrence of a similar accident.

Tootle Heights Park was used as the venue for a community service of remembrance for those who died in the 1914–18 world war. The photograph at the top of the page shows the head of the procession turning into the park, and the other the assembled villagers during the ensuing proceedings.

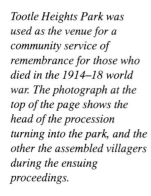

Eventually the disused quarry known as Fleming's or Railway was converted into a park and became a favourite venue for Longridge folk dressed in their Sunday best. A promenade on the Heights was enjoyable and not too taxing for the ladies in their heavy, voluminous skirts, and an added pleasure was the band concerts which drew quite a crowd. The smart uniforms of the band were complemented by the boaters, Eton collars and knee-breeches of the men, the broad-brimmed hats,

53

neat pigtails and long flowing skirts of the women, and not a bare head in sight.

And what better place to raise the union flag in 1915 for a recruitment drive for soldiers to replace those lost in France. A few years later a long procession led by the union flag wound its way through the village, along Higher Road and turned into the Tootle Heights Park where a remembrance service was held. A conspicuous banner read, 'To the Fallen Heroes, Remembrance, Love – Lest We Forget'.

Thomas Fleming

ANY account of Tootle Heights must mention Thomas Fleming who, in his day, was described as 'The Father of Quarry Masters'. One can do no better than quote from Tom Smith's description of this man:[6]

He never intrusted the inspection or superintendence of his workmen to anyone. Hence it was, that when gentlemen from other towns, architects, builders, contractors, and others, required to see him, it was common enough for them to find him working away in the rock, or at the crane, utterly indistinguishable from the other men employed under and around him. A suit of clay coloured trowsers or breeches, and a pair of clogs, was often enough the garb in which he has been found by some of the wealthiest and most talented men of the day.

In 1821 he was extensively engaged in supplying from his quarry those large blocks of freestone for such public buildings as were then in course of erection. About this time he made the acquaintance of the late Mr Jesse Hartley, the talented and able Surveyor of the Liverpool Dock Company, with whom Mr Fleming did considerable business. Many colossal blocks were conveyed from Mr Fleming's quarry to the docks at Liverpool. The enterprise and perseverance of Mr Fleming could, perhaps, never be placed in so favourable a light as at that period. There were no railways to connect the distant town of Liverpool with a remote village, and the only mode of conveyance was by horse. The thing seemed disheartening. Notwithstanding this, however the traffic was carried on in a satisfactory manner.

He was one of the promotors of the Longridge Railway. Mr Fleming was, however, rather tyrannical in his dealings with his workmen. He only paid them small wages, besides compelling them to patronise his 'Tommy shop' where they obtained groceries etc. at about 35 per cent above ordinary shop prices. But in this latter respect he was little better or worse than most of the other Longridge employers of his day. Mr William Marsden, Mr T. Spencer, and Mr J. Fletcher, all kept 'Tommy shops'.

The people of Longridge ought never to forget one who worked so hard and so successfully, as assuredly did Mr Fleming, to raise Longridge from being an obscure and insignificant village to a position of note in the stone trade.

Fleming Square, probably named after Thomas Fleming, quarrymaster and farmer, who lived close by, next to the Weavers Arms. His house was also a shop where, it is said, his workmen were obliged to spend some of their wages. Fortunately, since this photograph was taken in the early 1980s, the houses have been beautifully restored.

Whilst there is no doubt that Fleming is best noted for his position in the stone industry, some mention should be made of his farming activities. The Tithe Award of 1837 shows him owning twenty acres of land in Dilworth as well as being the tenant of a further fourteen acres in Alston. His house at that time was just off Market Place, in the square which is named after him, his Alston fields were close by, and his Dilworth fields were situated close to the present cricket field and in the Tithe Award are described as 'Marsh'. Mr Fleming seems to have tackled his farming with the same drive as his quarrying for the Preston Agricultural Society, in 1840, presented him with a prize of three sovereigns[7] 'for having drained in the most effectual manner the greatest quantity of land in proportion to the size of his farm with 2570 rods (of 7½ yds) of stone drains. The contrast is striking between his and some adjoining land in undrained state'.

The land in that area had always been known for its extreme wetness; during this century the late Mr Harry Newsham had difficulties when draining that area because of the presence of pieces of bog oak. So wet was it, that in the seventeenth century and earlier the usual route from Longridge to Chipping ran up the fell road and then dropped down past Birks, which was once an inn. Eventually a suitable road was constructed along the lower route.

Thomas Fleming died in 1861 at the age of seventy years. He was then living at 24 Market Place, which was next door to the Weavers Arms. Although success marked his business activities, tragedy stalked his private life: he lost both his wives, and all his children died before him.

The Stone Industry Workforce

WORKING with stone was an exclusively male occupation, where the work-force employed a variety of skills. Some of the men physically dealt with the rock at the quarry face, or split up the large blocks, some operated the cranes, steam shovels or other engines, some dealt with the loading of the wagons, some were blacksmiths, while others were masons who finally shaped the stone to order. Unfortunately the national census does not make clear the exact occupation of each of the men, but it does list them as working in some part of the industry. Using these statistics an analysis of their age range can be made by referring to them all as 'stoneworkers'. The figures used refer to those men living in the village. Very few came from the immediate surrounding rural area. It has not been possible to include those who arrived by rail from further afield.

In 1851 the industry employed a fairly even spread of workers from late teenage to almost fifty years old. It will be noticed that 3% were under fifteen years of age; the practice of employing such youngsters in the quarries had ceased by 1881. At this later date almost a quarter of the workers were between twenty-five and twenty-nine years of age; this group would best be able to cope with the hard physical work required. It is hardly surprising that there was a great reduction in workers over fifty years old, but those who remained were probably the skilled masons, or the engine operatives. In both 1851 and 1881 the average age was thirty-three years.

By way of comparison it is most interesting to study a similar analysis of another exclusively male occupation – the farmworker. Here the statistics refer to those living in Alston and Dilworth outside the village of Longridge. Although many women were employed at farms, the census returns suggest that they were probably working in the house or dairy. The graphs of male workers illustrate clearly that it was quite normal to continue working on the farm until comparatively old age. The patterns of the 1851 and 1881 graphs are basically similar, with fairly even spreads of workers throughout normal working life. The average age was forty-one years in both cases.

Further comparisons can be made by referring to a later chapter on the cotton industry in the village (see page 108).

Working in the Quarry

TOM Edmondson spent many years of his working life in the quarrying industry. He left school in 1906 at thirteen years of age and went straight to Spencer's Quarry which, at that time, was leased to Kay & Edmondson (his father's firm). When he was eighty-six years old he talked about some of the aspects of the industry:

'Where did you go to school?'
'Berry Lane with a man called Mr Dean.'
'Were you ever a part-timer at school?'

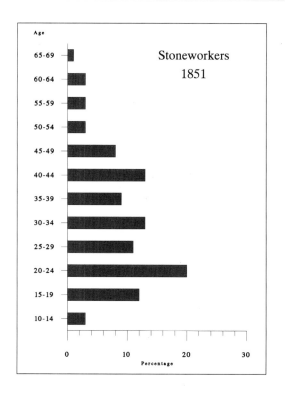

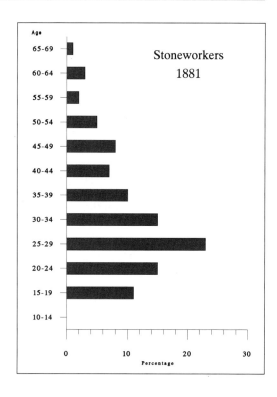

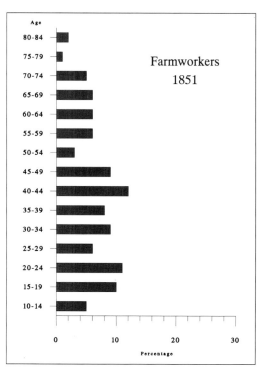

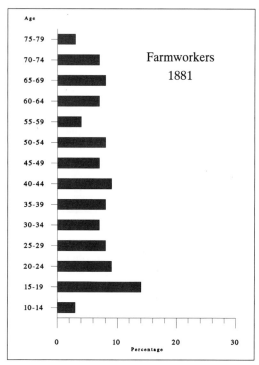

'Oh no! They did at the mill, but not into the quarry. They could go part-time at twelve at t'mill.'

'Did you go to straight to the quarry from leaving school?'

'Yes. Thirteen years old, I was. 1906.'

'What did you do when you went at thirteen?'

'It's surprising what they found you to do at thirteen. All t'rough, heavy work, you know. Moving dull picks to the smithy, and sharp ones out. And [coal] slack to the crane which was run by steam. And setts – they were making setts. They had to be moved into a shed to be finished off. You got to making setts and things like that when you got a bit older. Setts are six inch square stones. Some call them setts, some call them pavers. You know going up to St Paul's Church – they were a rough poor job. Not a tip-top job. In front of the Dog Inn there's some laid – a better job.'

'Did you have a blacksmith at the quarry?'

'At the quarry we'd a few blacksmiths. When I was about seventeen or eighteen this old blacksmith left and he'd been showing me a thing or two. My father told me, when the blacksmith left, 'What about t'smithy fire, Tom?' I was having a do at t'tools, you see. And I got to do 'em a bit better than 'im. For a start I must not have been doing too well, but we managed, and as time went on I got to be quite an expert at the job, with a bit of advice from a steel traveller who used to come round. I did a lot of blacksmithing in the quarry as I got older and more experienced. I would say my father had a few blacksmiths, and never one really mastered the tempering job. I don't think they did. I can remember, as a boy, a man took a sharp pick in. The blacksmith could see a great lump broke off it. He used another and another lump broke off it. He gets hold of it and sends it right into the smithy door. The blacksmith came out – I was 'appen fifteen or summat like that – he said, 'You want to be more careful using them picks. Don't be so rough with them.' He said, 'I know my job, but you don't know yours.' I didn't know then, but as years went on I found out he was right. That if he had tempered them properly they couldn't have broken, not like they did.'

'Did they use explosives in the quarry?'

'They used explosives a lot for moving the soil and thin layers of rock on the top. Then the stone goes thicker till it's thick enough for door jambs and heads and sills. Then, generally speaking, they cut it with wedges. They made a wedge hole, and after you had made your wedge hole with your pick, you run through the hole with a bottomer – they called it a bottomer – it was a narrow pick with a flat point – and they'd fine the hole out. The bottomer was sharpened very slender and fine, and the wedge that they put in would be at least a quarter of an inch thick at the end. When you put it in it didn't go to t'bottom o'th'ole. And you hit it wi' t'hammer. It tightened up. If it went to the bottom of the hole, when you hit it with the hammer it would just bounce out. And it was surprising how, if you made your wedge holes right and your wedge was right, how easy it cut. That was getting the big blocks without damaging them. It is quite a skilled job. Some men varied at making wedge holes as straight as a die. But the latter period as I was in the quarry they used plug and feather. They drilled it and

Chapel Hill Quarry, now the refuse disposal site. (Photograph courtesy of Lancashire County Library.)

then dropped in feathers. They were half round and thicker at the bottom than they were at the top. Then they knocked in the long, slightly tapered plug between the feathers. It saved making all these wedge holes by hand. It had a disadvantage. When it was cut with the wedges it were nice and straight. With the plug and feather it would leave a half round, but it was that much quicker that it saved time, and it was a lot easier.'

'Did you saw the big blocks into shape?'

'We hadn't a saw. Nook Fold had a saw, and Croft had a saw, and we sold them to Thomas Kay at Chapel Hill. He had a saw.'

'So you got out the big blocks and somebody else shaped them?'

'Yes. At Lancaster Town Hall there's a lot of pillars, and just for ornament's sake there's a square pillar and then one worked on the round – just for ornament. We made up a lot of stuff with a quarry pick and what they called a scappling hammer.'

'How many hours a day did you work?'

'Oh, when we started, forty-nine and a half, if it was a full week – weather permitting. But if it rained hard then it was impossible for them to work – they used to be rained off.'

'And no pay?'

'Oh, no! No pay. We used to average about – a man wouldn't need to lose any time – used to average in a year about forty-three hours a week.'

'What did you get an hour?'

'When I started they'd be getting eightpence an hour – that was old money.'

'That was the experienced man?'

'Yes, the skilled man. The unskilled man, if he was a good workman, got sixpence an hour. If he was getting on a bit and losing his strength a bit, and his ability, fivepence an hour.'

'Did most of the men come from Longridge?'

'Yes. There was quite a straggling come from Preston end. They used to come on the train. Used to get a weekly ticket. Used to cost them about fivepence a day, if they booked a weekly ticket.'

'What time did you start work?'

'Seven o'clock in a morning. Work finished at half past five at night. Half an hour off for breakfast, an hour for dinner. Now then in the depths of winter it was dark till eight o'clock and it was dark at half past four – sometimes dark before that. That's where men lost their time, in the dark weather. They worked from light till dark, and as it come lighter they worked longer.'

'Were there problems with water in the quarries?'

'Oh yes. A man called Joe Sharples worked Chapel Hill till about 1900. And then Crofts bought it. That was before my father took Spencer Quarry. There were two quarries there [at Chapel Hill]. Thomas Kay and this Joe Sharples. Well Sharples' quarry was on a lower stake than ours, and it flooded with water sometimes and he'd to pump it out, and when he pumped his out it left Kay's quarry nice and dry for nothing. It fell out that Croft bought it off Sharples. "Now Kay, you'll have to join me at this pumping!" said Croft. But Kay wouldn't join, so what did Croft do? He let it come up and it flooded Kay's quarry out. Then my father were foreman for Kay, and then they went into partnership as Kay & Edmondson and took Spencer Quarry. That quarry's been flooded ever since [Chapel Hill]. The Corporation [Preston] rented it off Kay for pitching for the reservoir, but they only worked it down to water level. They never did bother to do any pumping.'

'Did you have many injuries in the quarry?'

'We'd one fellow, John Johnson, he fell down t'cliff, and he didn't injure hisself so much. He let on his hip and his hand were under his hip and it broke his wrist. Otherwise he was only shaken up. But there was a man, Robert Seed, at t'other end, and it was in 1912, it was King George V's coronation, I think, he'd taken a bit of land there, off t'quarry, Seed and Cookson, and he'd gone at night, to bare a bit, and he was risking standing in rather a dangerous place. And there was me and another man called Christopher Harrison. Chris, he was older than me, I was about eighteen or something like that, and he says, "You're in a dangerous place there, Bob!" "I'm all right," he said, and I looked, and he was working away, and I looked again and he'd gone. I could swear he'd tumbled down. I said to Chris, "He's tumbled down!" and I run down and he was as dead as a duck stone. He'd let on his head, and he'd dropped on to a lot of big stones – head first. He'd been undermining it a bit so as it could fall off, and it had dropped a bit sooner and knocked him into t'quarry. But he was in a place where he shouldn't have been. He was working t'quarry himself, and he wouldn't have sent a man where he was risking it. He was risking it himself for a quick way of getting shut of the top muck.'

'So if you got a piece of land you were allowed to quarry it by yourself?'

'Yes. I'd just a little bit of land, and I'd rented that bit they called Croft End. There'd been a quarry there and another quarry next to it. Well that fellow had to keep so far off t'boundary, and this fellow had to keep so far off t'boundary. [When two quarries were adjacent work had to stop at least six feet from the boundary, thus leaving a wall of stone at least twelve feet thick.] Old Kay tried to rent it to t'Corporation and they sent a man to look at it. He said it was worthless. But I thought, "It's worth something, is that." And my father told me, "I think it'll turn out not so bad." It was at Chapel Hill, about 1926. My father had to close at Spencer so I took the little bit as it was all come into one owner's hands. I had it for about a couple of years or so, but I made a bob or two there.'

The Reservoirs

ALTHOUGH now in the Ribble Valley local government district, Longridge's physical position and geological make-up has, in the past, directed its fortunes more towards Preston for fulfilment. Its situation some 300 feet above Preston was exploited by the original railway which relied on gravity for its motive power with the stone laden waggons. The nature of the rock on which it stands was fully appreciated and exploited when so much building material was required in Preston and beyond. The stone which was used to commercial advantage in nineteenth-century Preston helped considerably in the subsequent growth of that town. The tens of thousands of additional families had to have that vital commodity, water, and so it was to Longridge, with its water-storage possibilities and its proximity to catchment areas, that Preston turned for an answer to its problem.

Prior to 1830[8] most of Preston's water supply came from the many wells which had been sunk. Public pumps were at the side of many streets, while some traders took water round in barrels and sold it by the canful. As the population rose from 12,000 in 1801 to over 30,000 in 1830 it was clear that the existing supply was hopelessly inadequate and none too healthy also. The Preston Waterworks Company which had been formed in 1832 set out its thoughts and hopes:

> Whereas the Inhabitants of the Borough of Preston and . . . the Township of Fishwick . . . are not at present well or conveniently supplied with water . . . being obliged to have Water conveyed to them in Carts . . . and liable to increased Danger . . . by Fire . . . the Township would be better preserved and protected if a constant supply of Water were provided.
>
> And whereas there are several Springs of Water called Eccles' Well, Walton Well, Chapel Well and Bolton Well, all situate in the Township of Alston-with-Hothersall, in the said County:
>
> And whereas a constant supply of water . . . might be obtained from the aforesaid Springs or Wells, and from other sources within the said Township of Alston-with-Hothersall, and also in the Township of Grimsargh-with-Brockholes . . . by conducting the water from such Springs

and Sources into proper Reservoirs, by means of Cuts, Drains, Tunnels, Conduits, Feeders and other Aqueducts and from thence by Pipes to the houses and Premises of the said inhabitants.

These springs were duly linked and directed into a storage reservoir on the east side of the Preston–Longridge road nearly opposite the junction with Gamull Lane. This was known as the Fulwood Reservoir, which was filled in in 1933. Further north, the Grimsargh Reservoir was completed in 1835, and about the same time the Dilworth Reservoir was constructed. Despite these efforts the new facilities could not cope with a further rise in Preston's population to 50,000 in 1841 and so a site adjoining Pinfold Lane in Alston was acquired. Here the first Alston reservoir (now No. 3) was built in 1842. Up to this time the water supply to the town was 'raw'; untreated in any way. Soon after, filter beds were installed at Grimsargh and several miles of conduit built to carry water from further afield on the Longridge Fell to the Dilworth and Alston reservoirs. Meanwhile the waterworks company realised that it had to increase its storage capacity further, as the population continued to soar. The site of a small storage pool at Spade Mill was acquired and the capacity increased considerably. The site also contained an inn, The Black Bull, the name of which was then changed to The Corporation Arms. This new reservoir, completed in 1862, came none too soon, as Preston's inhabitants then numbered almost 83,000, by which time it was imperative that the catchment area was expanded in order to increase the supply of water. Several years of work were required to lead water from the Hareden, Langden and Losterdale streams in Bowland. An adequate supply having been provided, it was then necessary to increase storage again to guard against a repeat of the drought which had occurred in 1868 and which had emptied the reservoirs. On this occasion, in 1886, the Alston reservoir was deepened increasing its capacity from eighty-four to ninety-six million gallons.

There then followed three years of drought which stretched the supply to the limit and prompted the purchase of the Alston College Estate which adjoined the Alston reservoir. The college buildings were demolished along with Crow Trees Farm and water was admitted to the second Alston Reservoir (now No. 2) in 1899. Work here did not go according to plan, as considerable problems arose with the southern embankment and finally, after much effort over several years, it was decided to leave the banks seven feet lower than originally intended and with a capacity reduced from an intended 275 million gallons to 183 million. Capacity was further increased in 1905 when Spade Mill was enlarged. Much of the excavated clay was carried by aerial ropeway[9] over Dilworth Lane and across the fields to help bolster the embankment at Alston No. 2. A year later the small Dilworth lower reservoir was constructed. In 1922 work began on another vast thirty-acre reservoir in Alston (now No. 1), but it was nine years before the work was completed as difficulties occurred again with the embankments. In the early 1930s work began on improving the aqueducts which carried the water from Bowland, requiring the laying of 10½ miles of thirty-inch diameter steel pipes and the drilling of two tunnels. The Whitewell tunnel, which is 618 yards long, contains the pipe and in that sense differs from the second. Locally, a tunnel was driven in a straight line for 1,016 yards right through Longridge Fell. The Dilworth Tunnel runs from near Jenkinsons Farm in Thornley to the Spade Mill site and was completed in 1934. Here the water flows through the tunnel rather than being piped, as there is a slight fall from the Thornley to the Dilworth end. During construction a two-foot gauge track was used with a battery electric locomotive operating inside the tunnel and petrol locomotives outside.[10] Indeed, narrow gauge tracks and locomotives were used in the construction of all the later reservoirs. Naturally, much local stone was used in lining the embankments: the Chapel Hill quarries supplied material for the Alston reservoirs, whilst an incline carried stone from Nook Fold quarry to Spade Mill. The last of the Longridge reservoirs to be built was Spade Mill No. 2 which came into use in the late 1950s.

		acres	millions of gals
Dilworth Upper	1835	7½	24
Alston No. 3	1842 (deepened 1886)	17	86
Spade Mill No. 1	1862 (enlarged 1905)	29	198
Alston No. 2	1899–1901	33	183
Dilworth Lower	1906	1½	7
Alston No. 1	1931	30	259
Spade Mill No. 2	1956		212

CHAPTER 7

Cottages and Cottage Industries

Club Row

THE origin of this terraced row of stone cottages was researched by the late
Eric Clarke, who found that at a meeting held on 6 March 1793 at the house
of John Swarbrick of Dilworth (The White Bull), it was decided to form a
society or club to allow a definite number of subscribers to obtain a
newly-built house.

It is often thought that this was a self-help scheme for the local quarrymen,
but this was not so. It was a speculative venture on the part of men who had
money to invest. Of the subscribers nine were yeomen (quite wealthy
farmers), four were weavers, two were stonemasons, and one each was a
carpenter, a shopkeeper, a clogger, a travelling dealer and a cotton spinner.
There is no evidence that any of the subscribers lived in any of the cottages.
Tenants were placed in the cottages and their rents paid into the club funds,
so that there was no financial advantage for early owners, and no disadvantage for those who had to wait almost ten years.

At the meeting 'Articles of Agreement and Rules' were drawn up and the
secretary, committeemen and trustees appointed as follows:[1]

Articles of Agreement for Building a House, with Necessary and Coal-
house for each Subscriber (according to a plan to be fixed on by a Majority
of Subscribers) entered into and agreed upon by us whose names are
under-written, at the house of John Swarbrick in Dilworth, this sixth day of
March, 1793.

Article First: A committee of three subscribing Members to be appointed by
a Majority of Subscribers, for the purpose of Contracting for land sufficient
for such Houses, and convenient gardens thereto, providing Materials setting the Work, letting the houses as they become habitable, and transacting
all business relative thereto to the best advantage of the Society. A Secretary
and Book-keeper also to be appointed by a Majority of Subscribers, for
entering all necessary Accounts, into a book kept for that purpose. Each
committeeman to have Sixpence allowed him each monthly meeting for his
trouble, with reasonable expenses for any journeys they may have relating
to the business of the society.

II. Each member shall deposit the sum of one guinea on signing these Articles, to be applied to the benefit of the Society; and shall on the first Saturday in every month, between the hours of seven and ten o'clock in the evening, attend the house of the said John Swarbrick and pay into the hands of such Secretary, the sum of ten shillings and sixpence, as the subscription of Club-money and three pence each for the expense of the monthly meeting. The Club-money to be deposited in a Box provided for the purpose with four locks, and lodged with the said John Swarbrick . . .

III. Any subscriber not paying up his subscription for the space of three months or upwards shall be expelled from the Society . . .

IV. Each house, or set of houses, shall be ballotted for at the time of letting: the Workmanship, and Proper Deeds made out for every distinct Proprietor, at the expense of the Society, and lodged in the Society's Box till the whole be completed.

V. Each member shall have the liberty to enter upon his own House, or put a tenant therein on a Rent to be fixed by the Committee, the rents shall go to the general fund . . .

VI. If any person during the Club hours shall become Quarrelsome, or be guilty of Swearing or Cursing, Laying Wagers, Promoting Gaming . . . such member shall forfeit the sum of one shilling, or on refusal of Payment to be excluded from the Society . . .

VII. Each Proprietor shall have a Covenant, inserted in his Deeds, not to lay or suffer his Tenant to lay, any Ashes, Dung, Manure, or other Nuisance, at the front of his own or any other House . . .

VIII. The Committeemen and Secretary shall be appointed annually on the first Saturday in April in every succeeding year, and continue in office for one whole year unless dismissed for neglect of duty or other misdemeanour.

[The Rev. Robert Parkinson, minister of Longridge Chapel of St Lawrence, was appointed secretary.]

IX. If any matter or thing for the Mutual Benefit ot the Society shall be proposed at the monthly meeting, the same shall be determined by a majority of Members present and entered into the Account book by the Secretary. But nothing shall be admitted tending to alter or destroy the external Uniformity or Regularity of the Buildings, which is inviolably to be adhered to.

X. For the better carrying the present Plan into Execution and to preserve Unity and Friendship amongst the Members, it is further agreed that if any subscriber shall divulge the secrets, or do anything to the Detriment of the Society, such Subscriber shall upon Conviction of a majority of Members present at the monthly meeting next after such offence, forfeit the sum of five shillings for the benefit of the Fund, or be expelled from the Society.

On the 4 May 1793 the members agreed to purchase from John Seed of Whittingham, late of Dilworth, yeoman, a plot of land 120 yards by thirty yards, as staked out from the front of two closes in Dilworth, near the village of Longridge lying east from John Seed's Inn, The White Bull, and in the tenure of John Swarbrick. From February 1794 until January 1804 construction work was carried out. The cost of each house was £138 3s. 6d.

This particular society or club is recognised as one of the first, if not the first, building society in the country. It was what was known as a 'terminating society', closing down when the project was completed.

Today it is commonplace for both husband and wife and older children to go out to work, but this was not the case in Longridge before 1850, when the first cotton mill was built. The ability to practise a system of dual economy depending on a cottage industry was recognised as an important requirement in the design of the Club Row cottages, and in many of the subsequent cottages built in the village. The cottages were provided with cellars into which a cotton handloom could be placed, and it was from this source that a second income was derived. At the end of the eighteenth century and during the first half of the nineteenth there was outdoor work for the menfolk on the land or in the quarries, but little scope for the women, so the acquisition of a loom was most welcome, and during this period cotton handloom weaving gradually increased in importance in the village.

King Street

IN 1798 while the Club Row Society was still in existence, a new society was formed with similar rules, the meetings being held in the house of Thomas Mackinson in Alston on the first Monday of each month.[2] Twenty-five members made up the society, some of whom also belonged to the existing one. Land was acquired on the 1 February 1800, from Thomas

These two houses at the corner of King Street and Dilworth Lane were demolished soon after this photograph was taken in 1972. The lintels on the ground floor suggest that, at some time, the windows were much wider. There also appears to have been a very wide door opening to the left of the archway. This is strange, because such an opening would have led directly into the acutely-angled corner of that room.

Smith of Preston (late of Blackburn), clogger, and conveyed to the Rev. Robert Parkinson, Christopher Nuttall, yeoman, and John Abram, inn-keeper, all of Alston, for £198. The land was a plot in a close called The Tidy, ninety yards by twenty-six yards, and another called Barn Field, in Dilworth, of 60½ yards by twenty-six yards. On this land the King Street houses were built. The total expenditure over the period 1799 to 1814 was £7,914 14s. 2½d., of which £1,090 8s. 5½d. was interest on borrowed money, making the cost of each of the twenty-six houses £304 8s. 3d. – well over twice the cost of the Club Row houses.

An indenture of 1815[3] states that Roger Fleming bought No. 11 and installed James Duckworth as tenant, and the presence of tenants in some of the other houses suggests that, like Club Row, this was a speculative venture by the owners. Here, too, the dwellings were adapted for cottage industry by having a through cellar with a window at both front and back. The front cellar windows have now disappeared as the level of the road and footpath was gradually raised, but a close look will reveal some lintels. At the rear of the houses the cellar windows are retained, along with flights of steps leading up to the ground floor. The cellars were able to take two looms, one in front of each window, thus providing maximum light for the opera-tive. Behind the houses were the outside toilets, and also some sturdy stone sheds in which nailmakers operated. In 1861 there was a post office at 10 King Street.

Langton Row

HOUSES at the top end of Dilworth Lane used to be called Langton Row. Oral tradition hints that the Row had, at one time, a rather unsavoury reputation which was centred on the presence of a 'doss-house'.

As far back as 1841 a lodging house was recorded in Langton Row, run by Catharine Eccles, who was probably a widow. Living with her were her four children ranging in age from two to fifteen years, and there were also four lodgers: a labourer, a cotton weaver and two tramps from Ireland. In 1851 and 1861 the house was in the charge of Jane Bibby, a widow, who had four lodgers in 1851 and five in 1861, all of whom were born locally and employed in the cotton industry. In 1871 there was a noticeable change when locally-born Jane Ashton ran the house. She had six lodgers, two from Ireland, and one each from Manchester, Seacombe, London and Matlock.

In every other respect, in the years mentioned above the Row was populated much like the others in Longridge. In 1871 it had seventy-seven occupants, fifty-one of whom were born locally.

Quite a change seems to have taken place by 1881 when the Row had a distinctly cosmopolitan make-up with only twenty-four locally-born amongst its sixty-seven inhabitants. Clearly locals were moving out and in-comers from far and wide were replacing them. The lodging house was then run by Edward McCullen who was born in Ireland, as was his wife, but two of their children were born in County Durham and one in Preston. Living with them were three grand-children named Murphy, born in Blackburn. Also, as lodgers, were three labourers, two born in Ireland and one born in Calcutta, India.

Next door, at No. 7, all four occupants were from County Durham. At No. 13 the head of the household and his wife were born in Ireland, and they had two lodgers, one from Lancaster and one from Dinckley. There were nine lodgers at No. 14, two from Ireland, one each from Wigtonshire, Bolton, Leeds, Liverpool, Manchester, Stockport and Westmorland. Others in the Row came from Hampshire, Devon and Stafford.

One wonders what part all these people played in achieving such unpopularity. Perhaps they did not conform to locally-held views or standards of conduct, or perhaps they were regarded with suspicion because they came from distant places and, as lodgers, were considered as rootless individuals. No doubt their gathering together in such a small area did not help.

The lodging house has long since been demolished, as indeed have other houses in the Row.

Nailmaking

IT is not known when the first nailmakers arrived in Longridge, but there are four recorded in the 1841 census. The most significant of these is John Schofield, who was born in Chowbent, near Atherton, an area to the south west of Bolton which was a nailmaking centre in the early nineteenth century. He was followed from the same place soon after by two other young nailers, William Prestwick, or Prestwich, and William Kay. Their expertise was, no doubt, passed on to the locally-born, for in 1851 there were nineteen nailmakers, twelve of them born in Alston or Dilworth. The trade continued to flourish, as in 1861 there were eighteen nailers. Although numbers fell to ten in 1871 and eleven in 1881, it is clear that it was still a significant industry.

It is probable that there were at least two nailmaking premises in Market Place or at the top of Fell Brow for this is where, in 1851, John Schofield employed five men, and where the four members of the Ormerod family operated. The Prestwich family lived in Langton Row (Dilworth Lane) and probably worked behind King Street. The workshop arrangement in Newtown was radically different in that the hearths were inside the cottages. The Newtown operation was run almost exclusively by the Almond family, five of whom were still working in 1881. John Schofield was still nailmaking in 1881, after over forty years in Market Place. William Prestwich combined nailmaking with being sexton of St Lawrence's Church. As he grew older he passed his business to his son, David, but continued as sexton and parish clerk. His second son, Nathan, was a nailmaker early in his working life, but later moved into Berry Lane where, in 1881, he was postmaster and ironmonger. Later the Prestwich hardware shop was next door to the post office (now an estate agent's). Tom Smith relates that William was notorious, in the middle years of his life, for his drunkeness,[4] though later he became a reformed character and an enthusiastic advocate of teetotalism. It is said that during his forty-one years as sexton he assisted at 1,755 funerals and dug the graves for most of them.

Handloom Weaving

SPINNING and the weaving of the resulting yarn are processes which have taken place on a domestic basis for thousands of years. Therefore it is not unreasonable to suppose that spinning and weaving took place in the houses, particularly of the farmers, in the Longridge area long ago. The production of cloth acted as a useful and probably necessary supplement to income as many of the farms were so small as to provide only a meagre subsistence economy. (In 1851, twenty-nine farms in Thornley had an acreage less than thirty, eleven of them less than fifteen acres.[5])

Edwin Hopwood[6] quotes an interesting account of the way in which handloom weaving developed in the home, particularly the farmhouse, in the eighteenth century:

> The farming was generally of that kind which was soonest and most easily performed, and it was done by the husband and other males of the family, whilst the wife and daughters and maid-servants, if there were any, attended to the churning, cheese-making, and household work; and when that was finished, they busied themselves in carding, slubbing, and spinning wool or cotton, as well as forming it into warps for the looms. The husband and son would next, at times when farm labour did not call them, size the warp, dry it, and beam it in the loom, and either they or the females, whichever happened to be least employed, would weave the warp down. A farmer would generally have three or four looms in his house, and then – what with the farming, easily and leisurely though it was performed, what with the housework and what with the carding, spinning and weaving – there was ample employment for the family. If the rent was raised from the farm, so much the better; if not, the deficiency was made up from the manufacturing profits.

Several seventeenth- and eighteenth-century documents relating to this area make direct reference to such processes. The probate inventories[7] for this area were almost exclusively of the property of farmers, but a study of over two hundred of them reveals surprisingly few references to the equipment which would be used. Perhaps, even at that time, it was more common to purchase readymade cloth rather than to weave one's own, or perhaps such equipment was no longer of use in the house of an ageing farmer and he had parted with it. These local inventories refer only to wool and flax, as cotton would not be generally available for the handloom weaver at that

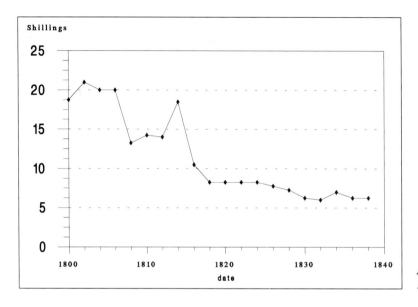

Average weekly wages of handloom weavers, 1800–38.

time. James Hacking of Alston, who died in 1671, had all the equipment necessary for producing cloth. He had: 'Reeles distafes with tow cards & the heckle : Yarne & flax [it is not clear whether or not any of this yarn was wool] : two pairs of loomes & measureinge instruments'.

The domestic process would begin by placing the wool or flax fibres on the tow cards and combing them with the heckle or hackle in order to align them. They were then ready for the distaff and spindle process which twisted the fibres together to produce the long lengths of yarn which would be wound on the reels. These operations were traditionally carried out by the womenfolk, especially the unmarried ones, hence the term 'spinster'. The resulting yarn provided the warp and weft for the weaving which took place on the loom.

The distaff and spindle was very slow in the production of yarn and was superseded by the spinning wheel. Although quicker, it still took six spinners to supply the yarn for one handloom weaver.

William Norcross of Alston (d. 1726) had 'three spinning wheels reels and wool cards'; Robert Riley of Alston (d. 1742) had 'a spinning wheel and a Reel'; George Sharples of Alston (d. 1690) had 'a pare of looms 2 spinning wheels and all thereunto belonging'; it is doubtful if Lawrence Cottam of Dilworth (d. 1717) used his spinning wheel as it was with 'an old chair in the turfe house'; Edward Rhoads of Dilworth (d. 1706) had 'one wool wheele and a pare of cards' as well as 'wool and Lining yarn and flax'; Henry Hayhurst of Dilworth (d. 1664) was a 'linnen webster and had 'canvas yarn linnen yarn whited yarn looms for a Linnen webster & other things belonging' as well as 'Linnen cloth'.

In the second half of the eighteenth century machines had been invented to spin cotton on a large scale and quantities of this thread became available for cottage industry. As the handlooms were scattered widely it was necessary for someone to organise the distribution of yarn to the houses, state what was required, collect the woven cloth and pay the loomers, usually on a piece-rate. This was the putting-out system.

Handloom weaving of cotton in Longridge probably began in the 1790s when the cottages in Market Place, Fell Brow and Club Row were built, and further developed in King Street in the early 1800s. These houses were deliberately constructed with cellars to accommodate looms. Later, in the 1820s, the hamlet of Newtown became another handloom colony, the loomshop here being on the ground floor. In the meantime weaving continued in the surrounding farmhouses and cottages.

Many of the loom operatives were quite young and thus assisted with the family income from an early age. Life has never been without its tragedies and the following newspaper report of August 1852 serves to underline this:[8]

On Wednesday morning William Dewhurst, weaver, only 13 years of age, the son of Richard Dewhurst, of Clap Gate, near the Derby's Arms, Thornley, was found suspended with a cord from the top of his loom, and was quite dead. No cause whatever is known for the rash act.

Whilst most of the looms were placed in cottages, David Nuttall had assembled several in a loomshop where spinning also took place, and which was recorded in the tithe schedule of 1837.[9] David Nuttall was the grandson of another David Nuttall who, in 1764, bought from Thomas Haighton the land which became known as the Wheatsheaf Estate.[10] The younger David built Dilworth House in the early 1830s, and also built and ran a water-powered spinning mill at Spade Mill.[11]

George Whittle[12] was born in Withnell and arrived in Longridge in 1838. His father was a manufacturer of handlooms. George learned much about the cotton trade by working in Manchester before coming to Longridge as a putter-out. On arrival he lived on Chapel Hill with James Hayhurst, but after a short partnership with him decided to organise his own business and became master of several workshops, as well as handloom colonies in Hurst Green, Goosnargh, Ribchester, Copster Green as well as in Longridge. One loomshop was in the old workhouse, which was on Fell Brow, and it is probable that the shop existed during the time that the workhouse itself was functioning. Goosnargh had a similar workhouse where, in 1831, a newspaper advertisement[13] called for: 'A steady man and his wife, without a family, required as Governor and Governess of the Goosnargh Workhouse. The man must understand Weaving thoroughly.' In both houses several looms would be operated by the inmates. They would certainly have had the time for this work, as the hours of labour at that time were 6 a.m. to 6 p.m. or during the hours of daylight in winter. Half an hour was allowed for breakfast and one hour for dinner. Both workhouses closed in 1839, the persons at Alston going to Ribchester workhouse and those at Goosnargh going to Woodplumpton.

Tom Smith relates[14] that George Whittle walked to each place once a week in order to recruit weavers and to meet the orders of the cloth merchants. This was at a time when factory production was in full swing in the Lancashire towns. In the late 1840s he was operating a warehouse near the crossroads at the bottom of Kestor Lane (See 'Fire at Mr Whittle's Works').

After 1800[15] the financial fortunes of the handloomers fluctuated wildly. Smith writes that between 1825 and 1830 'so well off were the handloom weavers that they frequently lit their pipes with 20s. notes. It was no uncommon thing for a female weaver to weave three 20s. "cuts" in a fortnight'. However, this situation contrasts with that reported by the *Preston Pilot* in 1846:[16]

In the districts of Mellor Brook, Balderstone and adjoining districts, the hand loom weavers are still suffering under the most grievous privations, with no symptoms of returning comfort. Many of the families are reduced to the lowest depths of poverty and in lieu of oatmeal for porridge bran has been substituted.

The following year saw a remarkable change as difficulties hit the mills. Again the *Preston Pilot* reported:[17]

We understand that this branch of manufacture [handloom weaving] is now in a more flourishing condition than it has been known for many years past. In many places in this neighbourhood, where the mills have ceased running, the operatives have availed themselves of this; and should the briskness continue, it will prove an advantageous change for them, as, on fancy goods, which are much in demand, as much as from twelve to fifteen shillings per week can be earned.

Despite these fluctuations the average weekly wage of the loomer had, in general, continued to fall from 1800. G.H. Wood[18] estimated that in 1800 the average wage was 18s. 9d., in 1805 23s., in 1810 14s. 3d., in 1815 13s. 6d., in 1820 8s. 3d., in 1825 8s. 3d., in 1830 6s. 3d., and in 1835 6s. 3d. But throughout this period the weavers of Longridge seem to have fared better than the average.

CHAPTER 8

Newtown and its People

N EWTOWN is the name given to a small group of terraced houses situated on the east side of Preston Road, near to the junction with Chapel Hill. At first glance Newtown is not impressive – just a group of nineteenth-century terraced cottages on the outskirts of Longridge. Its significance is not appreciated until one sees it in relationship to the rest of early and mid-nineteenth-century Longridge. This development, initiated by the local doctor, rapidly increased the size of Longridge by over 20%. It is difficult now to imagine that these houses once reverberated with the clatter of shuttles and the ring of the hammer at the forge, hordes of children played, shouted and quarrelled, and handloom weavers gossipped at the pump.

Origin

THE origin of this community (named because, at the time of its construction, it was separated from Longridge village by a quarter of a mile of fields) is closely associated with the farm, Hacking Hobs, which lies on the opposite side of the road. A brief history of Hacking Hobs is, therefore, relevant to an understanding of Newtown.

The late eighteenth century saw the building of many houses on Fell Brow, Market Place and Higher Road, as evidenced by several datestones. King Street was begun in 1805 and completed during the next ten years. Club Row was erected during the last ten years of the nineteenth century. Newtown was born in 1825 and completed between 1835 and 1840. Prior to 1850, therefore, Longridge was a very small hamlet consisting of a group of houses around the parish church, a linear development of stone houses on the fell road and the outlying community of Newtown.

Clearly, before 1750 practically the whole of the area consisted of fields, and associated with this land were the farmhouses. The farmers were obviously wealthier than their workforce and built houses which were designed to last and to display the owner's status. The labourers' cottages which were, no doubt, much meaner buildings, have long since been demolished. Many of the local farmhouses were rebuilt in the eighteenth and nineteenth centuries but, fortunately, a few of the older ones still remain:

Crumpax (1596), Hacking Hobs (1608), Daniel Platt (*c*.1615), Old Dun Cow Rib (1616) and Sharley Fold (1619) are all fine examples of late sixteenth- and early seventeenth-century construction. It is possible that Berrys Farm is older than all of these as it is cruck-framed and was probably thatched originally.

The datestones of Crumpax and Old Rib are still visible, but at Hacking Hobs the original entrance and datestone are concealed by a more recent lean-to extension. Above a pleasant Tudor style doorway is fixed a plaque bearing the legend:

1608
T D
E

This suggests that the builder's initials were probably 'T E' and his wife's 'D E', and a study of contemporary local family names makes it a strong possibility that the surname was Eccles.

In 1673 the house was referred to as 'The Platt at the Hobbs'[1] 'platt' usually meaning a bridge. Tom Smith, in his *History of Longridge*, records that on 20 May 1673,[2] the farmers of Alston agreed to pay for road repairs. The signatories of this document included Thomas Gregson and, as the farm was definitely in the possession of the Gregsons later, it is probable that this Thomas was the owner in 1673. The Gregson and Eccles families were closely related; Seth Eccles was the owner prior to his death in 1724. All three executors of his will, in which he was described as a yeoman, tanner, were Gregsons – Thomas, John and George – and accompanying this will is an inventory of his possessions.[3] His cattle were valued at £19 13s. 4d. and his five horses at £15 10s.; his farm equipment was valued at £6 17s. 8d. and the animal feedstuffs at £13 17s.; all the household furniture and equipment amounted to £56 1s. However, the following two items are quite startling:

all the bark	£166 10s. 0d.
all the dry leather and the leather in tanning	£207 7s. 0d.
[Oak bark was an essential ingredient of the tanning process.]	

Seth was also owed over £53 by several persons. The total of his inventory amounted to £547 5s. 0d., which was a considerable amount of money, bearing in mind that the average inventory totals of Alston farmers at that time was £52. Clearly, the wealth of the farm came from tanning, not husbandry.

There can be no doubt that the owners of Hacking Hobs were very wealthy when considered in the context of the locality. The property passed to Thomas Eccles who died in 1777 and left the farm to his brother, Edmund, who in turn left it, on his death, to his son, Seth. It would appear that Seth was quite an important figure in the life of Alston. He and his predecessors were Roman Catholics. They were men of substance. Seth was a member of the select vestry[4] – a body of men selected to administer the affairs of the township at local level.

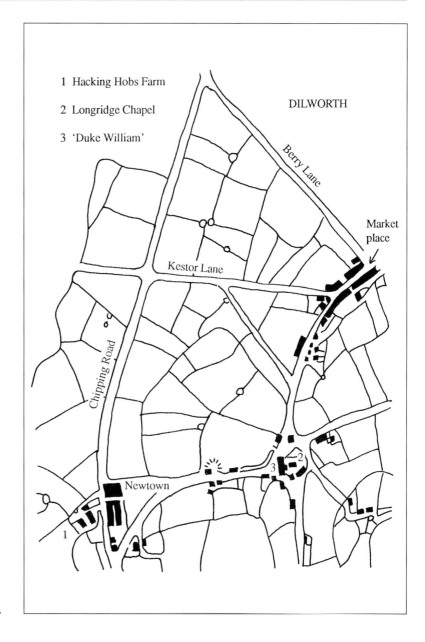

1 Hacking Hobs Farm

2 Longridge Chapel

3 'Duke William'

DILWORTH

Berry Lane

Market place

Kestor Lane

Chipping Road

Newtown

Longridge in Alston in 1837.

When Seth died in 1823 he left a considerable sum of money. His will reveals that he had been carrying on the business of tanning like his ancestor one hundred years previously. His principal bequest, the estate, he left to his son, Thomas. He left sums of money to his other sons, John, Seth and Edmund, and Edmund also received thirty perches of land on which to build a house. To his daughter, Margaret, he left bed and bedding and an annuity. To his wife, Elizabeth, he left an annuity as well as use of the parlour and room over the kitchen. It was usual in those days for a widow to be left accommodation in the family home.

The plot of land which was given to Edmund was on the opposite side of the road from Hacking Hobs. At that time the road was called Chipping Road. Edmund, like one of his brothers, decided to make a living outside farming and to go 'into cotton', whilst his brother, John, studied medicine at St George's Hospital, Hyde Park, London.[5] Unfortunately this young man died of typhoid fever at the very beginning of his career, and this prompted Edmund to desert cotton and follow his brother into medicine. It was as a young doctor, therefore, that Edmund Eccles returned to Hacking Hobs. He was 36 years old when his father, Seth, died leaving him the land across the road.

Edmund was born in 1787 and, as a young lad of eight years old must have seen the beginning of the building of Club Row at the top end of the nearby village. Later, as a young man, he would see the construction of the King Street houses. In 1815 cottage industries were a normal part of the domestic scene, so it was essential when designing houses to make provision for them, and in King Street this meant having a cellar which ran from front to rear with a large window at each end. This room was large enough to hold two cotton hand looms. The King Street development was complete when Edmund acquired his plot of land. His plans were ambitious: the building of a house for himself, plus a small hamlet. Along with William Hubbersty, yeoman, of Samlesbury, John Francis Clarkson, yeoman, of Grimsargh and Richard Swarbrick, butcher, of Dilworth, a trust was formed and the building commenced in 1825.[6]

The cottages of Newtown (probably named by the villagers of nearby Longridge) had to emulate King Street and be equipped to accept hand-looms, but there were no cellars in Newtown; the workroom was constructed as a through-room at the side of the domestic living quarters. In the weaving cottages, access to the workroom was from the living section, as direct access from outside was not considered helpful to the weaving process. There was no fire in the loom room and the floor was of earth. In the nailing workroom there was no direct access to the 'house' but a door front and rear of the workroom.

The majority of the hamlet had been completed by 1835 and consisted of twenty-six houses, including the doctor's. Basically, the design was of two rectangles of terraced cottages separated by a wide road, Pump Street. Each had an open passage down the middle, that of the larger south rectangle being known as The Backs.

On 18 May 1835 the Newtown trustees sold a plot of land to John Clayton, a gentleman of Preston, which was described as follows:[7]

All that plot, piece or parcel of land situate, lying or being at Newtown in Alston-with-Hothersall aforesaid, part of a field called 'Croft over the Lane' which said plot of land is bounded on the west by the High Road to Chipping, on the east by the High Road to Longridge tapering to a point at the Junction.

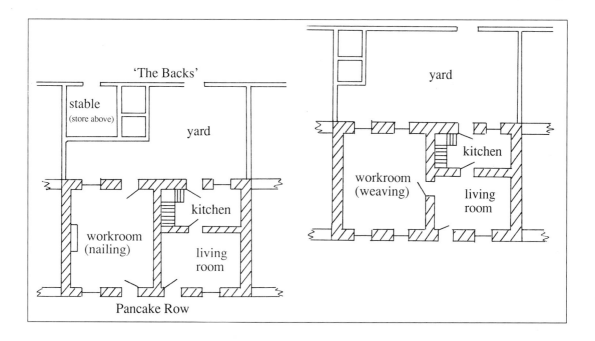

Labels within figure: 'The Backs', yard, stable (store above), yard, workroom (nailing), kitchen, living room, Pancake Row, workroom (weaving), kitchen, living room

Typical ground-floor designs of cottages in Newtown, with a workroom for nailing or weaving.

On that piece of land John Clayton built the Old Oak Inn, along with stabling, coach house and brewhouse. John Clayton died in 1847 and left the inn to his son, Thomas Dent Clayton. The inn is marked on the 1837 Tithe Map of Alston but, strangely, there is no mention of it in the 1841 census. Meanwhile the cottages rapidly filled and in 1841 were occupied by 158 people.

Whilst the building activities proceeded on Edmund's plot, problems seem to have arisen back at the farm. In 1832 Hacking Hobs was advertised for sale. As well as brief details of the farm and tannery, the *Preston Pilot* newspaper of 23 June 1832 printed the following:[8]

Notice is Hereby Given

That Thomas Eccles of Hacking Hobbs in Alston with Hothersall, tanner, hath by Indenture of Release & Assignment 17th May 1832 and made between Thomas Eccles of the 1st part, Thos. Boothman of Ardwick, gentleman, William Boys of Pleasington, gentleman, George Boys of Broughton, yeoman of the 2nd part and several persons of the third part whose hands and seals are set and subscribed (being creditors of Thomas Eccles) conveyed and assigned all his real and personal estate to those of the first part, their heirs, executors, administrators and assigns upon trust to sell the same and the money arising from the sale to be used for the equal benefit of all his creditors.

This report suggests that for some reason Thomas Eccles was in grave financial difficulties.

The Backs, Newtown, looking north. Above the door is a stone lintel which was above the archway which gave access from the Backs to the pump in Pump Street.

Handloom Weaving

THE majority of the Newtown workrooms housed two handlooms. The weavers obtained the weft on bobbins from the spinners, and loaded it into the shuttle which went from side to side between the warp. The warp or twist was not obtained on spools, but was supplied like a rope, rolled up, and called a ball warp. Usually the ball warp was already sized when acquired. Dressing was the process by which the already woven material was touched up. For the handloomer dressing was the job of the man who also straightened out the ball warp, combed it, removed excess sizing or added it where necessary. The Newtown weavers got a man called Dixon and his family to come from Bolton to do the job and he occupied what is now No. 5 Doctor's Row, with his workshop adjoining in the side road. Joseph Coupe, who died in 1975, remembered a beam fixed in the roof and openings through the two ceilings so that the warp could be stretched from ground floor to roof. Robert Coupe, who was born in 1836, was a handloomer and used to walk to Bamber Bridge for his ball warp and weft.

The handloomers had first claim on the smiths and nailmakers who lived nearby, as rapid repair of the looms was essential. From 1851 onwards there were both blacksmiths and nail makers in Newtown. The warehouse for storing the woven material was at the southern end of Pancake Row (10 Lodge View) and until about 1910 there were stone steps in the yard leading to a room on the first floor.

Although the number of handloom weavers remained high during the mid nineteenth century there is no doubt that from 1850 the trade of the handloom weaver was doomed. At this time the cotton mills of George Whittle at Stone Bridge and Hayhurst & Marsden at Crampoaks, Berry Lane, were beginning to operate. The last of the handloom weavers was Joe Watson (at 10 Lodge

The Backs, Newtown, looking south. The three tall buildings were behind the houses of the nailmakers, and were used for storing iron wire and nails.

View), and the last of the nailmakers was Jack Eaton in his cabin in the Backs, both of whom ceased their trades about 1900.

Nailmaking

BY 1851 nailmaking had joined handloom weaving as a cottage industry. In Newtown it was carried on principally by the two Almond families. At the rear of their cottage workshops the outbuildings were two storeys high, the lower room being used as a stable for the horse while the upper was used for storing the lengths of iron wire from which the nails were made. The cottage workroom was a smithy for nailmaking, but loom repairing had priority. As well as the ground floor forge, the flue fanned out in the room above to provide a wide forge space which was divided by bricks to allow four fires called 'hearths', allowing four smiths to work at the same time. Many of the nails which were made were called 'sparrowbills', a short nail up to an inch long used in footwear.

The workshop of William Almond was in Pancake Row. In 1895 Henry Coupe bought it from William Almond, a relative of Henry's wife, Ellen (*née* Almond). From the living room Henry made an entrance to the workshop, put a domestic fireplace where the forge had been, flagged the earth floor and made up the street door of the workshop by wall and window.

Materials could be moved in and out of the Backs by means of two entrances, one of which still exists, onto Preston Road or Chipping Road as it was called in 1851, and the other under an archway into Pump Street. This second entry was long since converted into a room, but as recently as the late 1970s the stone lintel of the arch was still visible from the Backs.

The original pump was removed during the 1939–45 war. The renovation of Pump Street was happily completed when this one, which was kindly donated, was erected in its place in 1981.

Pump Street

PUMP Street was so named, of course, because of the pump which was sited on the north side. No doubt the street was designed with a width of forty feet in order to allow room for horse-drawn vehicles to pass anyone using the pump. During the early days of Newtown the pump was the only source of water for the community, and it must have been the focal point of the hamlet, especially on busy Monday washdays as the housewives collected their water and passed on local gossip. It was not unknown for the doctor to escort a patient from the surgery round the corner to the pump in order to spray the cool, crystal water on to an ailing limb. The width of Pump Street made it the playground for the numerous children and the venue for the locally organised cock-fights and visiting entertainers. When water was eventually piped to each house the pump gradually became redundant, but it was not removed until the early 1940s, as part of the 'war effort'. In 1980 the hamlet was designated a 'General Improvement Area' and much work was carried out to restore it from its increasing dilapidation to its present pleasant state. The work was completed in 1981 when, in answer to an advertisement, a replacement pump was found to complete the restoration. Unfortunately, the vanity of the times has caused the name of the humble but respectable Pump Street to be changed to Southern Close.

As the cottage industries in the hamlet dwindled, many of the premises were split to form two dwellings, 2 & 3 Lodge View being an example of this. This explains why, for some considerable time, some cottagers shared an outside toilet with their neighbour.

The doctor's house

IT will be recalled that the first Dr Edmund Eccles built his house in 1825 on the corner of Doctor's Row. In May 1827 he married Elizabeth, eldest daughter of Richard Eccles of the Birks in Thornley.[9] He lived there until his death in the 1860s. His son, also Dr Edmund Eccles (1831–99), continued to live in the house after his father's death. The house was not only home for the family, but served also as a farmhouse with stables and buildings on the north side of Doctor's Row. The doctor employed a man to look after the farm and also to drive him in the trap on his medical work. The third Dr Edmund Eccles was born in 1879, but was not qualified when his father died in 1899 and there was, therefore, a break in the continuous medical service provided by the Eccles family, during which period another doctor practised from the doctor's house. Soon after returning to Newtown the newly-qualified third Dr Eccles moved into converted premises next door. Originally there was a grocery shop and two cottages at the north side of Pump Street on Preston Road, but in 1910–11 these were converted into a new doctor's house. Above a beautifully carved stone doorway are the doctor's initials, E E and the date, 1911. His widowed mother continued to live in the original house until her death in 1923, when Edmund and his family exchanged houses with his two sisters, who had been living with their mother.

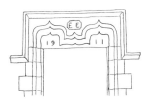

The doorway of the house of the third Dr Edmund Eccles.

The late Mr H. Bradshaw, who lived all his life in Newtown, recalled that when he was a lad he helped the third Dr Eccles:

> You used to carry water from the pump and I used to be errand boy for t'doctor. He used to make his own medicine. He had a dispensary, you know, and you used to have to carry water every night in big cans to t'doctor's and he used to use that water. He used to think there was nothing better. He had a farm as well and a coachman down at Spout House Farm and there was no telephone then. You used to come from school and sit in the surgery and then they'd give you errands to go. They had three horses – one for nights, one for days, and one for just relieving the other two – and you used to have to run down to that farm and tell the coachman.

It should be noted that as well as being benefactors of Newtown the three doctors played a prominent part in the life of Longridge. Certainly from 1825 to 1871 the first Dr Eccles was the only medical practitioner living in either Alston or Dilworth. The third doctor was blessed with two daughters, but no son to carry on the tradition after his death in 1937.

The Grey Horse

THE 1871 census records that a certain John Keighly, who lived at 8 Chipping Road, was a 'Beer Seller & Grocer'. His premises was also called The Grey Horse, but the local people preferred to call it The Galloper. It had a relief figure of a horse over the door and after No. 8 ceased to be a beer house Mr Joe Fletcher, a local builder, removed the horse and built it into the façade of the cinema, where it still resides. Incidentally, Joe Fletcher was born at No. 1, Newtown in 1861. He obviously liked eccentric decoration on his buildings, an obsession which is illustrated further by his work on the Swarbrick Arms (Empire Hotel) in Market Place, and Mercer's Travel Agency, at the bottom of Berry Lane, where terracotta tiles adorn the first floor.

Recent changes

THE fields which at one time separated Newtown from the village have now been submerged under housing and schools. Although, in 1970, it was an integral part of the expanding village, its prospects were bleak. Demolition was threatened. One house had already gone, others were in danger. Then economic difficulties and a more enlightened planning officer came to the rescue. It was realised that renovation was cheaper than renewal and, as is often the case in local government, financial considerations tended to outweigh aesthetic or historical arguments.

In 1980 Ribble Valley Borough Council declared Newtown a 'General Improvement Area' and much work was carried out to improve the appearance and services of the area. New pipes were laid, unsightly wires were hidden, attractive street lamps were installed, a stone bus shelter was erected, the streets were surfaced and landscaped and, to complete the picture, a pump was placed where the old one originally stood.

A clay pipe found during work on the G. I. A. scheme. Pipes like this would be used during the period between 1825 and 1840, when the buildings were constructed.

The name Pancake Row seems to have been rejected completely, although Pump Street is still permitted a mention on the street sign, albeit in a secondary capacity. One day the council and the residents may even agree to discontinue referring to the hamlet as the 'Southern Close Area' and revert to the historic name of Newtown.

Newtown reminiscences

IN 1979 Mr H. Bradshaw and his sister, Win, talked about their early lives in Newtown in the 1920s:

WB: 'There used to be a man as made oat cakes and they scrubbed the floor and used to put them on the floor, and they made treacle toffee as well.'

HB: 'And at this shop, when they turned it from a pub [The Grey Horse] they used to bake their own pies a t'back, meat and potato pies.'

HB: 'Down Lodge View they used to keep pigs.'

WB: 'Yes, across there, and make their own black puddings. They all had pens down Lodge View. There weren't them bungalows then. That was a big field where we used to go to play. And then there was what we used to call "the meadow". T'doctors used to let it out sometimes to the Coupes. And then there was a hill going up that little pad and they called it the "cut through". You were one big family in Newtown. It's not the same now. Old Mrs Hunt, she used to go round making them gruel and that when another baby were born.'

HB: And wesh their clothes and help one another.

WB: 'Send 'em round and get your hair done in curls. They put them in rags. There were some good old people – well they were old to us then.'

HB: 'And on the front here there were trees overlooking that road across there. There was a big orchard there belonging to Hacking Hobs Farm and in the summer all the old people used to take their chairs and stools and sit under – they were real summers in them days. When we were going to school you could take your shoes off and run about in your bare feet, couldn't you, Win?'

WB: 'We've always lived in Newtown, but we were born at No. 10 in Lodge View, and then we came here when t'war started – 1914. We'd only just come in that week and t'soldiers, they were marching 'em down.'

HB: 'To Weeton Camp, you know – Territorials from Longridge.'

HB: 'The chap next door here to our Win used to be a fish hawker, and he used to keep his pony at the back in a stable, and then there were another little place adjacent to that and he used to put his fish cart in there. Then Jimmy Whitehead used to keep pigeons over there, and he lived where Stan lives now.'

WB: 'My Uncle Joe had pigeons when he lived at t'pub [Grey Horse] with my grandma.'

'Where did they keep the pigeons?'

HB: 'At t'back and you can see the places yet. There's one at t'back of t'shop – it's an electrician's shop [not now]. Then there's one just behind me.'

WB: 'Then some gipsies once came to live there and they kept their horse in the house. In t'kitchen and fetched it out of t'front door and took it down Whittingham Road to put it in a field wi t'cart at t'back. They were grand people though.'

HB: 'They used to sweep the Backs every day.'

WB: 'They were lovely. It was one big happy family. The children all played together.'

HB: 'There were only one old lady who didn't like a lot of kids, and there used to be plenty, didn't there.'

WB: 'Well, they never did any damage. They used to play 'whip and top' and skipping ropes.'

HB: 'And going asking t'weavers when they were coming home at night, "Have you any cracker?" – to make a long swatch to put on your whip to play whip and top. Then the lads who went to work used to say at night, "Now then you've had your turn in t'day time," and they used to start playing football. Aye, they weren't a lot of trouble in them days.'

WB: 'You had to run down to Alston Lane School. There were no buses and you took your dinner and they just had a coke stove.'

HB: 'To warm your tea.'

WB: 'If you were lucky to have a boiled egg they put it in the tea to warm it.'

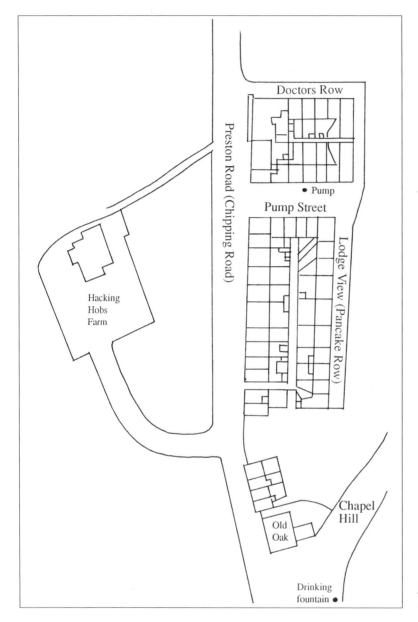

Doctors Row

Preston Road (Chipping Road)

• Pump

Pump Street

Lodge View (Pancake Row)

Hacking
Hobs
Farm

Chapel
Hill

Old
Oak

Drinking
fountain •

*Newtown as it was about
1932.*

HB: 'I'll tell you what, you know them new houses that they've just built across from Whittle's Mill, well there was a siding there and they used to come from Longridge and shunt wagons into that siding and there were big cranes and they carted all the stone from Chapel Hill and they used to load 'em in this siding. And Almonds used to do a lot of stone work across from St Wilfrid's and they used to fetch their stone down into this siding. [Almonds were stone masons and had their yard in Derby Road.]'

'Did you use the train for getting to Preston?'

WB: 'Yes, it was a treat to go to town and it was only 5d. half fare and a lady used to take me and one of her girls.'

HB: 'You went to t'Towneley up that pad and got on there at t'station.'

WB: 'After we left school we used to go down on the buses on Saturday afternoons and have a look round the market and do any shopping. Then we had tea in town, and went to the pictures, first house.'

HB: 'In them days you went down to t'Old Oak, and there used to be rings on the wall. There used to be a captain come from Fulwood Barracks and we used to hold his horse. He used to go in and get a beer in a big glass container. "Hi, Beauty!" he used to say, "Come on now, have your ration." And he used to give this horse the beer.'

'Did they used to fasten the horses to the rings?'

HB: 'We didn't let 'em. We used to be there quick. Some were a bit greedy. They used to get at th'hook. A lot of these farmers used to buy horses and they used to come to Longridge Station and they used to drive them down like cattle from the station. Duxbury from Grimsargh used to buy a lot, and he'd be half kettled, hard hat on, and t'cigar, and he'd pull in and you'd grab th'horse. When he came out he'd say, "Have you looked after my horse?" He'd give you a penny and then he'd be away down t'road.'

'Who used to live at Hacking Hobs?'

WB: 'At one time Fred Bradley took it on.'

HB: 'Now then, you're going to laugh – he were a greedy fellow. If you went off what were t'footpad down t'field he'd chase you off.'

WB: 'You hadn't to pick a bit of firewood.'

HB: 'Or mushrooms that used to be in there. He watched 'em all, but he didn't ger 'em.'

WB: 'He had a lovely orchard.'

HB: 'Them big victoria plums – he didn't get all of them, you know. We'd let him get interested in milking . . .'

WB: 'And t'lads 'd be over t'wall pinching his apples.'

HB: 'T'policemen 'd come round and he'd say, "Now lads!". Used to walk down, did t'policeman.'

WB: 'But they knew he were coming.'

HB: 'He used to have that cape on his shoulder, and if he saw you congregating, "What's going on here?" and he'd clout you across th'earhole wi' t'cape. They were t'boss. I remember one time we'd bought a packet of Woodbines. They were five for a penny and we decided we'd only smoke one Woodbine at a time so there were five or six of us round t'back – we were smoking this cigarette, and who should bob round t'corner but this fellow named Catterall. "What the hell's going on here?" he'd say. "C'mon, let's have them cigarettes." And he'd take these four, and then he'd walk down t'road and we'd follow him, because there were all fields across there – no Hacking Drive. He couldn't smoke on duty then, you know. He used to have a quick 'n at t'bottom of th'back field. Smoking our health! But they were happy days!'

Saturday at the Pictures

THE late Mr H. and his sister, Miss Win Bradshaw described a typical Saturday afternoon:

HB: 'Saturday afternoon we used to go to the pictures and you could get there for a penny, and you had to put your name on a paper, and then at th'interval they used to put on their gas lights, you know. "Quiet!" he'd shout, would this big fellow, Tomlinson. You could hear a pin drop. He were supreme, you know, and he said, "*You* won't be coming in here again. *Out!*" and he'd kick you out if you misbehaved. Oh, he were t'boss. And then when they'd turned t'lights up they'd go on t'stage and they'd draw this paper out, and you'd get a bar of chocolate if your name came out lucky. Only a penny and it would be a 2½ hour show.'

WB: 'And they used to get these pictures where they were continued.'

HB: 'Fletchers owned it, but Tomlinson used to run it. He were t'chucker out and he didn't stand no messing. He used to sit on this corner smoking his pipe. A big fellow. He'd be six foot two or three.'

WB: 'A penny for t'pictures. You were lucky on Saturday and you had a good afternoon.'

HB: 'Then you used to go to t'chip shop for a ha'p'orth of chips in a little bag. At t'side of t'pictures at the end of the row in Market Place. Counsells used to have it. They used to sell ha'penny bags straight out and with peas that were a penny.'

WB: 'It were a penny if you had a shandy. They called them shandies – it were chips and peas.'

HB: 'They had this pan boiling up wi' peas in.'

WB: 'If you only had a ha'penny you could get a ha'p'orth of chips and put a lot of vinegar on and drink the vinegar after.'

Every cloud . . .

THE late Mr H. Bradshaw talked about his early working days and the unusual and profitable opportunities which came his way as a result of a coal strike.

I was t'first in t'family that didn't go half-time. I was thirteen when I went to t'factory, 'reaching'. It was Whittle's Mill. I didn't like that job, so any road, I packed it in after about twelve month and I went to 'moulding' at t'foundry serving my apprenticeship. I was on brass moulding. I was on core making at first. It was at Belmont Foundry. At first I went on iron. You had to make cores for casting iron. Then off that you went on t'flue on to brass. Then t'coal strike come on so it closed down. It would be 1926 when t'foundries closed. Couldn't get no coal. So I stayed there till that strike come on and of course everybody come off.

Now there was a pipe track coming through here – Hughes of Lancaster

– and this particular day I thought, 'I'll have a walk and see if I can get a job.' It was the fifty-four-inch main from Thirlmere to Manchester. It come across Whittingham Road. I went up and he said, 'Ah! you're too young for navvying.' So he said, 'I'll tell you what, could you brew tea?' I said, 'Yes.' So I got a job brewing tea, and do you know, I used to put milk in all their cans and I had more money than the navvies had. He used to say, 'Come on, get your cap out.' You got your cap out and you'd stand there and it seemed cheeky at first, and t'foreman 'd say, 'Come on 'ere, look after this lad.' And you used to boil these buckets of water – made a trench fire, you know, but when it come heavy going trench fires weren't so good, so we had to get a boiler, and do you know I got more money than they were getting. I used to come home and count it in there and, you know, some of 'em give you a shilling and a shilling was a lot of money in them days. And I used to go across to Ashley Lane to Daisy Bank. Dicky Bond kept th'Horns in Goosnargh then. They used to say, 'Fetch us a pint, nipper.' And you'd go wi' t'bike and a sack and get these bottles of beer and they'd give you tuppence for fetching bottles o' beer, and it were all in your time, you know. And then after, they used to chuck 'em over t'top – some was on piece work and they'd chuck their bottles over t'top – and you used to go wi' t'sack collecting empty bottles up and you'd get a penny a bottle. Do you know, honestly, I were making more money than what t'men were. They used to fetch their bacon – they were marvellous fellows, you know. They can say what they like, them spades as they had, they used to have 'em that clean they used to cook their bacon o'er t'fire on them. They were spotless, you know. Some had billicans and they'd put their billicans over this fire and brew their tea, and they'd make their own bacon and cracking their eggs, and some of 'em would wash their shirts in t'hot water on a Saturday morning. They'd wash their shirt and put it over what they called t'struts. They lived in Preston. They'd take 'em down on a wagon. They had a light track, you know, and they used to have these little motors and they used to take 'em down to t'yard. They put a siding for them, did Hughes of Lancaster, and t'train came up from Grimsargh and stopped there and they all got off and then they used to take 'em up to t'job, as far as Barnsfold. They were really grand fellows.

Then they sent back for me from t'foundry. They offered me 25s. a week, and I said, 'Oh, no. I've been making a lot more than that for brewing tea.' I were getting 39s. a week for brewing tea, and I'd be making £5 a week nearly some weeks. I bought two suits of clothes and an overcoat and shoes while I were there. It were good money, you know, for a lad.

CHAPTER 9

The Railway

ALTHOUGH few traces of the railway which ran from Longridge to Preston now remain in the town, there can be no doubt that it was the railway that made Longridge what it is today – a flourishing small town in a delightful rural setting. The popularity of Longridge stone in the early nineteenth century for public buildings, industrial enterprises and housing in the rapidly-expanding cotton towns of the county has been mentioned earlier. It soon became apparent that the normal mode of transport in the early 1800s was quite unsatisfactory for the movement of a heavy and bulky material. The seven-mile stretch of road to Preston was rough and uneven at the best of times, and horse-drawn wagons could make but slow progress. Indeed, three horses were able to move a mere three tons of stone each day to Preston. Large numbers of horses were required to ensure a steady flow of material, which still proved insufficient to meet demand, and a railway was the obvious answer. A committee was set up in 1835 to consider this venture, and the following year The Preston & Longridge Railway Bill was passed through parliament and received the royal assent.[1] The railway, which was to be horse-drawn, would have its Preston terminus at Deepdale and from there would run directly into the Tootle Heights quarry at Longridge. At the end of 1837 land had been acquired, the directors having declared themselves 'willing to deal liberally with landowners whilst resisting extortion'. Work was in progress on earthworks, bridges, culverts, and so on, and in April 1838 the *Preston Pilot* newspaper recorded[2] that the directors were in little doubt that the whole work would be finished by the end of the year. It was expected that the contractors would be able to increase their workforce by employing 'handloom weavers who are out of work and scarcely able to obtain food'. However, progress proved slower than hoped and Mr Wilkie, one of the contractors,[3] 'was urged to greater exertion to finish the portion of line comprised within his contract which the directors cannot but regret has so long exceeded the prescribed time.'

At long last, in April 1840, an advertisement addressed to 'Quarry Owners, Stone Masons and Building Contractors' declared:[4]

> The directors of the railway beg to inform the public in general that the line will be open for the carriage of stone, other goods and passengers on Friday,

the 1st day of May. As the tonnage for the carriage of stone is fixed at a low rate it will be well worth the attention of those persons who are in the habit of using stone for building, draining and other purposes. A carriage for conveyance of passengers will leave Preston for Longridge every Wednesday and Saturday morning at half past seven o'clock and return from Longridge at half past eight o'clock. In the afternoon it will leave Preston at four o'clock and return from Longridge at five o'clock.

The following were advertised for letting:[5]

Several spacious yards adjoining the Terminus of the railway at Deepdale Road – well adapted for the use of stone masons, builders, coal dealers who wish to carry on their business on an extensive scale. The railway will be able, from May 1st, to bring the stone into their yards. Plans may be seen by applying to Mr Bray, the owner or Mr J. Webster, the Secretary to the Railway Company.

The railway was designed to take advantage of the difference in elevation between Longridge and Preston, the loaded waggons being able to proceed downhill under the influence of gravity while the horses travelled behind in special vans. Their major function was to haul the empty waggons back uphill to the quarry. The following week the *Preston Pilot* commented on the forthcoming opening of the Railway:[6]

This interesting event will take place next Friday when large numbers of people are expected. The railway presents a somewhat singular feature being a continuous inclined plane so will supercede the use of steam. The return to Longridge will be effected by horse power. However if the undertaking be prosperous the gigantic aid of steam will in all probability be had recourse to. We sincerely wish all possible success and we think that as a mode of transport for stone, lime and other products of Longridge and vicinity it will afford incalculable advantages to the public of Preston and neighbourhood.

The auspicious opening ceremony was described thus:[7]

Yesterday (and a beautiful May day it was) was fixed upon for the opening of the railway from this place to Longridge, a distance of something more than six miles. It had previously been intimated that conveyances would be prepared for directors and friends. Second class carriages were prepared as the weather was favourable and some of the best horses, decorated with ribbons, from Mr Wilcockson's stud, he himself being the whip. A very comfortable number of persons were assembled and 'all right' being announced the carriages moved at a good pace to the Plough Inn, Grimsargh. It had been arranged to stop there to watch a train of waggons, stone laden, come down the steep incline, and afterwards the directors' carriages arrived at the terminus. After remaining at Longridge an hour whilst Mr Fleming's stupendous delf was visited as well as the one belonging to the railway, the carriages moved off as if by magic, Mr Bushel, the engineer of the line, acting as brakesman. He limited the speed to 8 m.p.h. to avoid accident and then to 20 m.p.h., half the speed it would have gone if the brake had been released. A mile from Preston the speed decreased and the horses which had followed at some distance were attached and so they arrived at Preston without accident. Three hearty cheers were given. Many people had assembled on bridges and were astonished to see the carriages move without power. A party of directors and friends dined at the Castle Inn and spent the evening most sociably drinking 'Prosperity to the Longridge Railway'.

In order to gain access to the Tootle Heights quarry a tunnel was constructed under Higher Road, while the other, higher quarries brought their stone down to a loading platform on the west side of the tunnel where a crane was used to load the wagons. The base of this crane still remains on John Smith Park and, although the tunnel is now blocked, the archway entrance can still be seen. On the keystone are the letters, P & L R (Preston & Longridge Railway), 1839 (date of completion), F H P (H. Parks, engineer), C + T (Cooper & Tullis, builders).

Although not on Tootle Heights, it should be mentioned that stone from nearby Lord's Quarry (owned by Lord Derby) was conveyed on a narrow-gauge line to a platform opposite Billington's Farm where it was transferred to a branch of the main line. The sharp bend into the quarry prevented the main line from proceeding further than the farm.

Whilst this new means of transport enabled far larger quantities of stone to be moved to the Deepdale yards where masons shaped it to order, the line proved equally popular with the public especially on public holidays. The *Preston Pilot* reported:[8]

> We noticed in our last that the directors arranged extra trains on Whit Monday. Parties availed themselves of quick transport to and from the upper end of the line. Others went by early trains for a day's ramble on the hills to enjoy a view of the beautiful and almost unlimited variety of scenery which presents itself from the heights above Longridge, there being no less than 418 conveyed along the line. Some trains came down the steepest part of the incline at nearly 40 m.p.h.
> Fare 4d. each way.

The comments in 1841 were even more encouraging:[9]

> Amongst the various ways of spending the holiday [Whit Monday] there has not been a more rational one proposed than that of a trip to the beautiful heights of Longridge from whence, should the weather prove good, the view of wood and water cannot be exceeded in the kingdom embracing as it does an immense extent of country bounded in the far distance by the sea. The facilities have been much increased since the opening of the Preston –

Longridge Railway. The journey home (six miles) has something of a novelty if we consider that the rate is from twenty to thirty miles per hour without the aid of horse or steam.

In 1843 work had commenced on the New Barracks at Fulwood, the contractors, Messrs Bellhouse & Co. of Manchester, taking the Railway Quarry and working it themselves for the required stone.[10] In fact the new buildings were used as an advert for Longridge stone:

> The Directors have the satisfaction of informing the Proprietors that the quarry belonging to the company, at Longridge, now occupied by Mr Bellhouse of Manchester, turns out quite to the satisfaction of the Directors, the stone got therefrom being well adapted to all kinds of building purposes. No better specimen etc. need be alluded to than the very extensive new buildings already erected for the New Barracks in Fulwood, the whole of the stone used therein having been got from the Company's quarry.[11]

Despite the encouraging public announcements, all was not well with the company. Profits fell far short of those anticipated and so it was decided to seek a buyer. An offer came from a new company, The Fleetwood, Preston and West Riding Junction Railway. As the name suggests, its intention was to link the West Riding of Yorkshire with a port development at Fleetwood. The Preston & Longridge Railway would be leased at an annual rent, a link from Deepdale to the Preston & Wyre Railway would be constructed, and a branch line would leave near Grimsargh and pass south of Hurst Green into the valley of the Ribble, cross the river near Mitton and proceed to Clitheroe and on to Skipton, where it would join the proposed Leeds & Bradford Extension Railway. Most inviting reasons were put forward for its probable success:[12]

> In connection with the North East Railway, this line will also throw open the watering places of Harrowgate and Knaresborough and the rich and beautiful scenery of Bolton Abbey and Wharfedale to the health and pleasure seeking denizens of Lancashire, while in return the shores of Fleetwood, Blackpool and Lytham and the romantic district of the Lake County, will be brought within the easy reach of the population of Yorkshire and Durham.
>
> The Lime Beds in the vicinity of Clitheroe furnish the best quality of Lime Stone in Lancashire, while the pastures of the Craven Valley are the well known resorts for the purpose of fattening for the markets of the manufacturing towns the cattle constantly imported from Ireland.
>
> The line will also afford great facility of access to the valuable Stone Quarries on the Longridge Fell, the purchase of which is included in the agreement for the Preston and Longridge Railway.
>
> Interested parties were cross examined on their views of the new railway. Amongst them was the Principal of Stonyhurst College which had 300 students and was within one mile of the line.[13] He felt that, 'The railway

would lower the price of coals and provisions, and confer other advantages, although he might regret it as destroying the picturesque features of a beautiful country. As a rich agricultural district it must derive advantage from the interchange of products with the manufacturing'.

An appropriate Act of Parliament was passed in 1846. The link from Deepdale was constructed and a start made south of Hurst Green by the digging of a cutting 250 yards long. The project was then abandoned when links on the east side of the Ribble were clearly not going to materialise, but the cutting is still a very prominent feature.

Meanwhile the day-to-day activities of the railway continued, but were rudely interrupted in January 1846 when, as the *Preston Pilot* reported, a most unfortunate accident occurred:[14]

An accident of a serious, but we are glad to state, under the present circumstances, not likely to prove of a fatal nature, befell a man on this railway, on Monday last, of the name of William Crook, a stonemason by trade, who was returning from Longridge to Preston, accompanied by his employer, John Parsons, and another man. It appears that all three individuals were seated at the front of a stone waggon, laden with stones, and that when they arrived at no great distance from Preston, the stone on which Crook was seated gave way and fell upon the rail, which caused him to fall also, and he reached the line in so unfortunate a position, as to have got his leg under the stone, which the moving waggon wheel continued to push forward for some distance before it could be stopped, and in so doing crushed the limb in a very serious manner. After being extricated, he was brought on to the Ribbleton Bowling Green public house, and Mr Booth, surgeon, was immediately called in, who, after examining the limb, declared at once the absolute necessity of an immediate resort to amputation, which was complied with, and the operation was performed by Mr Booth, in a most skilful manner, and we rejoice to add so successfully (judging from the present favourable appearance of the case), as to warrant the strongest assurances of the patient's perfect safety from any fatal results from the accident.

We understand that John Parsons had a very narrow escape from falling off the waggon, the stone upon which he was sat having also given way; and he was only enabled to save himself from falling off, by seizing hold of the lock of a heavy box, which had been fortunately put upon the stones in the waggon.

Even before the railway opened in 1840 it was recognised that the use of steam locomotives was an inevitable aim, but it was not until 1848 that an engine was purchased.[15] A celebration was planned for the first journey, and in its form far exceeded that of May 1840. It was graphically described by the *Preston Pilot*:[16]

We mentioned last week that the directors of the Fleetwood, Preston and

*The level crossing,
Berry Lane.*

Longridge railway station.

West Riding Railway had concluded on making the first public trip with a locomotive engine, furnished by Messrs Mould & Co., up the line, to give an invitation to their friends to join the party. Whit Monday was fixed for the fete, and about two hundred ladies and gentlemen (including a large party of officers of the 89th) joined in its celebration. Eleven o'clock was the hour of assembly at the Deepdale Road station, and shortly after that time the whole of the party were in attendance, and having taken their seats in the different carriages, the engine, (named The Addison, in compliment

The Crossing, Berry Lane, Longridge, (Lancs)

The crossing, Berry Lane. To the left of the gates is the signal box, and further left is the coal office of Thomas Banks & Co. On the opposite side of the road, to the right of the gas lamp, can be seen a wooden hut, and it was here that Mr Alston carried on his business as photographer. The site is now a small landscaped garden. The chimney of Crampoaks Mill was a prominent feature, as was the tall mill building to its left.

to the esteemed and indefatigable chairman of the company) which was decorated with several Union Jacks, etc. and a most handsome banner, bearing the inscription 'The Fleetwood, Preston and West Riding Railway' was attached to the carriages, and the signal being given, the train was soon in motion, and going at a speed very different from that which had been attained on the railway on the old system. As most of our readers are aware, there is a steep incline for a very considerable portion of the distance (in some parts one in forty five), so that the speed was occasionally relaxed. The admirable band of the 89th, which the commander of the regiment had most handsomely allowed to attend, were in the first carriage, and played some lively airs while on the journey. The train having arrived at the Longridge terminus, the party formed in procession, and preceded by the band, marched through the village (to the great wonderment of the inhabitants) to a large inclosure belonging to the company, and from which a most varied and beautiful view of the whole county might be had, and though the extreme distance was somewhat hazy, yet there was sufficient to be seen to satisfy the most fastidious.

A large marquee had been placed on the ground, in which was the lunch, got up with the greatest possible taste (and in which was included everything that was good and palatable) in our neighbour Mr Billington's usual satisfactory manner. One o'clock was the hour named for commencing operations, but as it was found that that time would be rather too early for mine host, a ramble was proposed, and various parties were formed to climb the heights, and obtain, if possible, a better and more extensive view. Several parties went to peep at one of the immense reservoirs belonging to the Preston Waterworks Company, on which were majestically moving two large and beautiful swans – others were wending their way to Tootle Heights, to enjoy the scenery, and thus the time was filled up till the parties returned to 'the field'. By this time, due preparation having been made, the party took their seats, the accommodation consisting of two ranges of tables the whole length of the marquee. It was found, however, that these would not accommodate the whole number, so that only about one hundred and fifty sat down – Thomas Batty Addison, Esq. and John Paley, Esq. occupied the head of each table. As we have said, the refreshment provided was most ample and substantial, as indeed it had need to be, after a long stroll in the bracing and pure atmosphere of the Longridge Fells. The corks of the Champagne bottles flew out almost as rapidly as the reports from the muskets of a body of soldiers firing a *feu-de-joie*, and the exhilarating beverage soon had the effect of imparting life and hilarity to the partakers of it. A reasonable time having been taken by the party to discuss the edibles, a considerable portion retired to make room for those who had had their patience tried during the while.

Speeches and toasts followed, and then:

A proposition was now made for a Quadrille upon the beautiful green turf, and no sooner proposed than adopted, the beaux and belles arranging themselves, when the elivening strains from the band were the signal for the dance, and the various young ladies with their delightful partners soon tripped it lightly and airily to the astonishment of the villagers, who had been drawn to the spot on hearing the music. Country dances and polkas followed, and were heartily enjoyed by the ladies and their gallant partners. As all pleasure must have an end, so had this delightful rural fete, and after regaining the road, the procession was again formed, and preceded by the band, retraced their steps through the village to the station, and having taken their seats in the carriages, were soon on the way to Preston, where they arrived without let or hindrance, or the least accident having happened, perfectly delighted with the treat which the Directors had so handsomely given them.

Despite the seriousness of its purpose the line was looked upon in some quarters with a certain amusement. This probably arose because the transport of passengers was of secondary importance and therefore had received less financial investment than many passengers would have wished. There is no doubt that the company had limited resources and could only purchase well-used engines and rolling stock. All these factors inevitably led to some derisory or tongue-in-the-cheek letters to the press, and two such appeared in the *Preston Guardian* in 1849.[17]

A cast-iron boundary marker of the Preston & Longridge Railway.

THE LONGRIDGE RAILWAY – SHOULD CATTLE AND
HUMAN PASSENGERS TRAVEL TOGETHER

Sir, – On Wednesday last I took it in my head to visit Longridge, and after depositing sufficient amount of capital to satisfy the functionary in Deepdale Road who supplies travellers in that direction with passports, I received my ticket and proceeded to the platform, which I promenaded as well as I could for a few minutes. An intimation being given that 'time was up', I scrambled into a carriage, first class of course, when to my surprise I found a quadruped in the shape of a fine calf, stretched within the compartment. Several other passengers noticed the same, and remonstrated thereat, but were given to understand that the practice was a common one, the Longridge directors being no respectors of persons clean or unclean, indiscriminately. Our journey, however, was not deficient in interest, for what with the wheezing puffs of the old asthmatic engine, the bleatings of the cow's daughter (for it was a wye), and the imprecation of an old gentleman whose juxta-position with the calf appeared a grievous source of annoyance to him, we had music enough to spare. Now, Sir, the Longridge line is one in which I have a deep interest, – first, because of the magnitude and importance, – secondly because of its mystery, it leading (as Byron says of the tide in the affairs of women) God knows where; and thirdly, on account of the independence it has displayed in resisting the blandishments of Hudson, who years ago had marked it for his own, and in standing out firmly against the introduction of Greenwich time which robbed above one half of the Kingdom of a clear ten minutes. On these and other accounts I had a deep veneration for the Longridge line, and therefore I was extremely sorry to see so dirty and obnoxious a practice as that referred tolerated in the travelling arrangements. Would it be too much to suggest that a separate box of some kind should be provided for the swine, kine, etc. which are conveyed on this railway? I should have no objection to contribute my mite for such a purpose, if the finances of the company are not equal to the task. The ride on the Longridge railway is said to be very interesting, but with such companions as I have named in the carriage the scenery cannot be enjoyed, or if any gratification does attend the excursion, it must be sheer animal gratification. Beside where is the distinction to be drawn? If calves are to be located within a passenger carriage, why not cows; and if cows, why not bulls; and if bulls, why should Mr Wombwell, if ever he thinks of visiting Grimsargh or Longridge with his establishment, be denied the requisite accommodation for a rhinoceros or boa constrictor? The precedent is a dangerous one, and may grow into a great abuse.

PRESTON AND LONGRIDGE RAILWAY – NEW ERA[18]

Sir, – I have often to my sorrow, noticed in your columns reflections of the most serious character upon the Preston and Longridge Railway. Nothing connected with that small but important line, has been safe from the attacks of malicious correspondents. First the Directors have been upbraided, and the secretary lampooned; the carriages have been caricatured; next the engine has been condemned; on another occasion the station and platform have been villainously reviled; and one audacious wretch has even gone to the lengths of disputing the accuracy of the time served on the railway, which, he contended, was infinitely inferior to Greenwich, and in flat contradiction with the sun. Without inquiring into the justice or injustice of these charges, and without referring to the faults, errors or deficiences of the past, I hasten to inform you that alterations and

One wonders which way this dog was travelling on 6 October 1913; perhaps it was to Longridge. Fortunately its owner failed to hand over the ticket.

improvements are being made as will effectually stop the mouths and pens of all complainants and eventually enable the 'Preston and Longridge' to take up a conspicuous position in Bradshaw's Guides, the share lists of the day, and public estimations. I am informed on the best authority – a half brother to the porter – that no less than four fresh carriages and two engines have been obtained, of the stock of the defunct Lancaster and Preston Company. Whether the Preston and Longridge succeeded to the above, by will or by purchase, I do not know; but certain it is that all these novelties, with the exception of one of the locomotives (which, to use its own words, 'refuse to be exiled'), have made their appearance on the Longridge line. The carriages are painted green outside and yellow inside, and have roofs, buffers and everything complete. They are to be divided into first, second and third classes, so that the plebeian and aristocrat may in future have their respective places, and that hideous system of republican equality or communism which has hitherto prevailed on the Longridge line (and which, on some occasions have even been carried so far as to lead to the admixture of bipeds and quadrupeds in the same carriage) will be done away with. The platform, also, is to be widened by 5½ inches, and I have been confidently informed that the erection of a new shed for passengers is seriously contemplated by the directors. To these great improvements I would take the liberty of adding, by way of recommendation, that a time-piece should be procured. A decent clock may now be had very cheap or might possibly be won at a raffle for a mere trifle. This desideratum being obtained, and the lad and man belonging to the company be placed in something like a uniform, the Preston and Longridge line might then appear before the world in its due importance. Permit me to desire Mr Editor that you will, in fairness give publicity to the improvements that have already been effected, and to express a hope that these proofs of the enterprise of the directors will remove all grounds for cavilling for the future.

Whatever the eloquent, letter-writing public might have thought of the railway, there can be no doubt that the conversion of the line to steam operation in 1848 was the beginning of a new era in the life of the village. Longridge had long had a tradition of cottage industry in the form of cotton handloom weaving, and the putters-out were quick to appreciate the possibilities offered by a new system of power which could haul weighty materials uphill to Longridge in a way which horses could never do. Cotton mills were flourishing in the ever-expanding nearby towns. Once coal in quantity could be moved to Longridge the way was open for the construction of steam-powered cotton mills in the village, the first of which opened in 1850. Immediately below Stone Bridge, loading areas for the mill as well as for the Chapel Hill quarries were built.

The failure of the ambitions of the F.P. & W.R. Railway Co. eventually led in 1852 to its inability to pay its annual rent to the P. & L. Railway Co.[19] The latter, in lieu of rent, acquired the engines and rolling stock of the former company, bringing about its bankruptcy. During the succeeding years, although the finances of the operating company were not entirely satisfactory, the day-to-day working of the line proceeded and only received extra attention from the press at the time of untoward events such as accidents, or the threat of them. In August 1867 the *Preston Pilot* reported an accident, the cause of which was established as negligence on the part of railway staff:[20]

A very serious collision took place on Saturday last, on the Preston and Longridge Railway. On the day named, the number of passengers was exceedingly large, caused by the annual guild and club walks at Longridge. The last train but one was despatched from Longridge about a quarter to nine o'clock, and proceeded all right till it arrived at Fulwood, where the tickets had to be collected. When the officials had just done collecting them, and the train had begun to move, the last train which had left Longridge a short time after its predecessor, was observed to be coming down the line with a rapid speed, but it could not be checked before a frightful collision had taken place. Several carriages were smashed and rendered almost useless, whilst the injury to passengers was very considerable. The scene was one of great confusion, and there being no lights at command, made matters worse. The injured were attended to at once, and a messenger despatched to Preston for surgical assistance. The number hurt was between 50 and 60. Fortunately no bones were broken.

Early in the following year a platelayer from Dilworth was tragically killed at the Fulwood station.[21] He had alighted from the train in order to have a conversation with a colleague, when suddenly he became aware that the engine had been whistled and was moving off. He ran quickly along the platform in order to climb aboard the train but, in some inexplicable way, he fell onto the line and was run over.

Of the many tragedies occurring on the railway none is more poignant than one at Christmas in 1859:[22]

It appears that a number of children were attracted to the level crossing of the line to hear the strains of a band of music which had been perambulating the village, and while they were thus engaged, a waggon of coals which had been shunted on to a siding, struck a boy six years of age, passing over one of his legs, stripping the flesh, and breaking the leg in two. Mr Eccles of Longridge, surgeon, was summoned to the aid of the sufferer, and it being deemed necessary to amputate the poor boy's leg the operation was accordingly performed, but the lad is since dead.

In March of 1868 there was quite a disturbing headline in the newspaper:[23]

ATTEMPT TO UPSET A TRAIN ON THE LONGRIDGE RAILWAY
William Wignall, provision dealer, of Lancaster Road, was brought before the Magistrates on Saturday morning last, charged with having attempted to upset a train on the Longridge Railway on the previous afternoon, by placing some railway 'chairs' on the line. Evidence was given as to the finding of the obstruction on the rails and the detection of Wignall within a few yards of the place where there was not any footpath or thoroughfare. The prisoner was committed to the Assizes, bail being refused.

Despite the tragedies and commercial setbacks, the line proved highly satisfactory in catering for the leisure pursuits of many of the inhabitants of Preston. At the end of August 1858 probably one of the largest invasions of Longridge took place:[24]

On Saturday last, the scholars of the Parish Church and All Saints' Sunday Schools, accompanied by their superintendents and teachers, visited Longridge. The monster party (numbering over 1,500) were conveyed in three trains, and on their arrival at Longridge, the scholars and their friends

Longridge from Tootle Heights in the early 1920s. In the foreground is the entrance to the railway tunnel which passed under Higher Road to the quarry beyond. On the extreme right of is a small crane, used to load wagons, and in the centre is Wellbrow Farm (now demolished), with its access road from Higher Road. Beyond the farm is Robert Smith's Victoria Mill, opened in 1862, and its two mill reservoirs. To its left is Crampoaks Mill chimney.

This building stood on the site of the present Stonebridge Surgery. It was at the side of the railway, and was associated with Whittle's Mill across the road. (Photograph courtesy of Mr B. J. N. Edwards.)

enjoyed themselves in various ways. Bands of music accompanied the party, and thus added to the pleasure of the day's excursion. All the party returned home in safety in the evening.

The laws of our country regarding Sunday trading are, and seem always to have been, confusing and perplexing, as a rail passenger found in 1859:[25]

... we reached our journey's end, and a halt of half an hour at the Townley Arms prepares us for the stroll higher up in the country. We cannot stay much longer, for here the foolishness of the enactment as to Sunday trading has made itself felt; we know we are 'travellers', but the moment the bell tolls for church we must away. Because a number of fellows all over the country have disgraced themselves by getting drunk on Sunday, all of the rest of mankind must be treated as drunkards too.

During the remainder of the nineteenth century the line was well occupied with the carriage to Longridge of coal, cotton, raw materials for the foundries and agricultural feedstuffs and machinery. The diversity of commodities carried necessitated the construction of quite complex sidings on the north side of Berry Lane so that the products of the local industries, along with stone, could be efficiently removed to Preston. The second decade of the twentieth century was marked by a rapid decline in the fortunes of the railway. As well as problems associated with the first world war, this period saw the almost complete demise of the stone industry as bricks became the principal building material. The development of motor transport, and along with it the improvement of roads, dealt a further blow. In order to counter this decline and maximise on the line's eastward projection, plans were devised to extend the line beyond Longridge to Hellifield via the Loud

Valley, Whitewell, Tosside and Wigglesworth. Again, this attempt to build an east-west link failed to materialise. Passenger traffic fell with the advent of regular bus services and ended in 1930 and the line finally closed in 1967, with a lone train making a farewell visit to collect rolling stock on 5 March 1968.[26]

It will be recalled that the line began in the ownership of the Preston and Longridge Railway Company and was then leased to the Fleetwood, Preston and West Riding Railway Company, soon to return to the parent company on the liquidation of the F.P. & W.R.R. In 1856 a re-formed F.P. & W.R.R. purchased the line and ran it until 1866, when it was taken over by the Lancashire and Yorkshire Railway. From 1867 until 1923 the line was run jointly by the L.& Y. Railway and the London, North Western Railway (L.N.W.R.). It then became part of the London, Midland and Scottish Railway (L.M.S.) until British Rail took over in 1948.[27]

This chapter has provided a brief summary of the history of the railway, especially in its early years. Much use has been made of the columns of local newspapers both to provide contemporary accounts and also, perhaps, to illustrate the Victorian passion for expansive descriptions. Those who wish to read a more complete history along with technical details should consult Norman Parker's excellent book, *The Preston & Longridge Railway*.

CHAPTER 10

Mills and Factories

Cowley Brook

THE village of Longridge had to wait until 1850 before manufacturing processes were power-driven, but long before this a series of water-powered mills were operating along the banks of Cowley Brook.[1] This cheap, re-usable power source operated Moor Hey Mill, then Knowle Green Higher, Knowle Green Lower (Bridge Mill), Clay Hill Mill, Lum Mill, White Carr Mill and Cage Mill: all involved, in one way or another, with the textile industry. Manufacturing on this scale required a local workforce which was conveniently housed in the many cottages that once lined the valley. In 1841 there were seventy-nine inhabitants of cottages at Lum Mill alone, apart from an equal number upstream.[2] Amongst these was a constable, needed, perhaps, to deal with a workforce reported to be in dire need of religious direction.

Lum Mill, which was by far the earliest, followed by Knowle Green Higher, were originally allied to local agriculture and operated as corn mills.[3] During the second half of the eighteenth century there was a great increase in the local cottage industry of cotton handloom weaving, and also the beginnings elsewhere of cotton powerloom weaving; processes limited by the speed at which the cotton could be spun into thread. Inventors such as Arkwright, Crompton and Hargreaves put their minds to this problem and eventually produced various types of spinning frame which could be powered by waterwheels. These machines vastly increased the quantity of thread so necessary for the weaving process. It was clear to local entrepreneurs that involvement in the growing textile industry was the way to a profitable future. The earlier Cowley Brook mills were converted and the later ones built for this purpose. Lum Mill, Knowle Green Higher and Lower Mills began operating spinning frames,[4] while the others concentrated on producing the bobbins needed to cope with the increased amount of thread being produced. Later Knowle Green Lower became an iron foundry producing rollers required in improved methods of spinning. Its name was changed to Bridge Mill and it was run by Richard, William & James Bond. The Bond family was well known locally and ran foundries at Chipping and also at the Poplar and Belmont works just outside Longridge on the Inglewhite Road.

Eventually it was found that water-powered mills could not compete with the newer steam-powered machinery and so, one by one, the Cowley Brook mills closed. Spinning and roller-making ceased in the 1860s and bobbin-making near the end of the century. Interestingly, some of the mills then returned to meeting agricultural requirements by producing hay rakes and other items which needed a wood-turning process. All the mills had ceased operation by the early years of this century except Cage Mill, which continued wood-turning until the 1970s.[5] During the early years of the nineteenth century there was considerable felling of woodland in this area, many of the advertisements for the sale of this timber directed at the Cowley Brook enterprises and recommending its use for bobbin-making.

In 1826 Lum Mill was the subject of a 'church brief' as a result of a disastrous fire in October of the previous year when the bobbin and wood-turning works was completely destroyed. Such was the loss sustained that a national collection was organised. Such collections were recommended to the crown by the local justices of the peace. The crown then issued an order or 'church brief' stating that the particular distress should be announced in every church throughout the land and collections made for the relief of the sufferers. A complete transcription of the brief appears in Appendix A of Smith's *History of Longridge*.[6] Church briefs were discontinued in 1828.

An interesting case concerning one of the spinning mills was heard at the county court at Preston in 1856. It was unusual in that an employee sued his employer and won, and was reported thus:[7]

A Nice Specimen of a Cotton Lord
Dawson v. Aspinall

Plaintiff who is a card-master, summoned the defendant, a manufacturer at Knowle Green, for the sum of £1 16s., two weeks wages. It appeared from the statements of the plaintiff that he had been engaged by the defendant as a card-master at his mill, at 18s. per week wages. After being in his employ ten weeks, and getting all right and straight, the defendant discharged him without a moment's warning, saying that another man had offered to fill his situation, and take charge of the throstle-room besides, for 16s. a week. – In answer to His Honour, Mr Aspinall said he had no printed rules hung up in his mill; that he never gave a fortnight's notice, and never received such notice from the hands who left his employment. – The Judge said it was the rule to give and take a fortnight's notice; Dawson must have justice. – Order made for the amount claimed.

The mill referred to was probably Knowle Green Higher. A 'throstle' was a type of spinning frame.

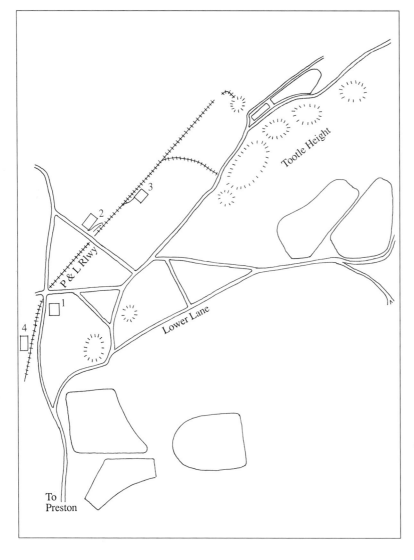

Longridge cotton mills:

1   *Whittle's Mill,*
    Stone Bridge Mill
2   *Crampoaks Mill*
3   *Victoria Mill*
4   *Queen's Mill*

Factories come to Longridge

GEORGE Whittle was quick to see the potential of the steam locomotive-operated railway which commenced in 1848. Heavy goods such as cotton and coal could be brought uphill from Preston to Longridge and therefore, with readily-available water, all the requirements of a powerloom mill could be met in Longridge. It was particularly important to establish such a factory, for the handloom weavers were cruelly exposed to competition from the weaving mills of the nearby towns. Indeed, in 1838, at a directors' meeting of the Preston & Longridge Railway, when work on the construction was discussed, it was stated that:[8] 'The contractors will be able to employ

Stone Bridge or Whittle's Mill. The row of houses at the front of the mill was originally called Silver Street. The railway, in its cutting, bisects the angle between the roads. (Photograph courtesy of Longridge News.)

handloom weavers who are out of work and scarcely able to obtain food.' It was thus that in 1850 Whittle built the first steam power-operated cotton factory in Longridge close to Stone Bridge after which it took its name. It was carefully sited near the railway, where a platform was built to assist the loading and unloading of materials. In many areas of Lancashire there was considerable opposition from the handloom weavers to the new factories, but this was not the case in Longridge. It is probable that, as Whittle was so well known in the community and lived in the village, his proposal was accepted as a means of providing a security of employment that was becoming increasingly difficult to maintain for the loomers. At that time Whittle was living at the top of Fell Brow, and living with him was his nephew, a young man of twenty-two years called Robert Smith, an assistant to the cotton manufacturer.[9] Initially plain cloths were woven on Lancashire looms, but later fancy cloths were produced on jacquard looms. In 1925 the mill had 602 working looms. It closed in 1961.

In 1851 William Marsden and James Hayhurst built Crumpax (Crampoaks) Mill on a green-field site in Berry Lane. Again, William Marsden[10] was a putter-out who had come to Longridge in 1832 and was, therefore, well known to the community; as, of course, was Hayhurst. A short branch line ran directly to the factory. Both spinning and weaving took place at this mill. At the end of May of that year The *Preston Pilot* reported:[11]

On Friday week Messrs Hayhurst and Marsden, manufacturers, Longridge, celebrated the rearing of their new and extensive power loom shed. A liberal supply of bread and cheese and ale, etc., was supplied to the workmen who had been engaged in the erection of the buildings, and in the evening a number of Messrs Hayhurst and Marsden's personal friends sat down to an

An aerial view of Berry Lane showing the railway line, which crossed the road by means of a level crossing. Prominent in the centre of the picture is Crampoaks Mill, built in 1851 and closed in 1959, which had its own branch line from the railway. The mill site is now taken up mainly by the Spar supermarket on Berry Lane. (Photograph courtesy of Longridge News.)

excellent supper provided by Miss Dewhurst, the worthy hostess of the Red Lion, to which ample justice was done. The company separated at an early hour, after having spent a most agreeable evening. We understand Messrs H. and M. intend spinning as well as weaving in their new shed.

As well as spinning the mill had, in 1925, 501 Lancashire looms. It closed in 1959 and was later demolished apart from the weaving shed which is now part of the garage in Berry Lane.

In 1862 Whittle's nephew, Robert Smith of Dilworth House, built Victoria Mill at the bottom of Green Lane. This factory could easily be served by the railway as the line to the Tootle Height Quarries ran close by; indeed the building was so close to the boundary of the railway company land that the drain pipes had to be inset in the wall. Here a branch loop line ran right through the building with the platforms under cover. In 1925 it had 650 Lancashire looms and forty Northrop looms. It closed in 1935.

In 1874 the fourth factory, Queen's Mill, was built, again sited adjacent to the railway. It was constructed of brick, unlike the other three which used Longridge stone, but it did use local clay which was dug and fired close by. It was different also in that it adopted the later style of mill architecture, having a round cross-section chimney instead of the square of the other three. A further difference was that it was owned by shareholders and was registered as The Longridge Manufacturing and Spinning Company Ltd., though it was known locally as the Co-op Mill. Queen's Mill wove fancy cloths for dresses and curtains as well as material for corsets, and supplied the curtain material for the liner *Queen Mary* when it was launched in the mid 1930s. In later years the terylene curtains for the *Royal Yacht Britannia* came from the mill. A loom and a weaver were sent to the 1923 British

Leonard J. Lord in his design office at Queen's Mill in about 1930. Mr Lord designed patterns for curtain fabrics and shirt materials.

George A. Lord, winding master, with the beaming machine at Queen's Mill in about 1930.

Empire Exhibition in London. During both world wars the weavers received awards for their outstanding contributions to the war savings funds. In 1925 the mill had 552 looms. It closed in 1964.

As each mill opened it absorbed the existing workforce and required more. This led to the construction of the terraced rows associated with the cotton industry, initially on a small scale, with the building of Silver Street for the Stone Bridge Mill workers, but later the more typical patterns such as Mersey Street and Chatburn Road appeared. Silver Street was the name given to the row of sixteen houses between the crossroads and the entrance to the mill. In 1861 of the fifty-nine occupants of working age, forty-one of them worked at the mill.[12]

Labour relations were generally good, but a few exceptions have been recorded. In 1852, the year after the opening of Crampoaks mill, the following report appeared in the *Preston Chronicle* of 3 April:[13]

On Saturday last the weavers in the employment of Messrs Hayhurst and Marsden of Longridge stopped work for higher wages. A meeting of the hands was held on Monday, when they resolved upon terms which they would resume work. Their masters refused to accede to them, but on Wednesday many of them went to work at the old rate.

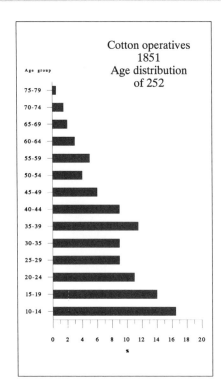

Cotton operatives 1851 Age distribution of 252

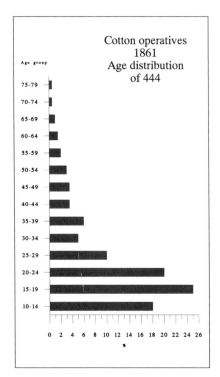

Cotton operatives 1861 Age distribution of 444

At the time of the 1851 census only Whittle's Mill at Stone Bridge was operating, and it is clear that the mill drew its workforce exclusively from those between ten and thirty-five years of age. There was a fairly even balance between the sexes, though the largest individual group of powerloom workers was of females in the 15-19 age-range. Only a small percentage of cotton operatives were powerloom weavers, however, and among the handloom weavers there was a greater percentage of females in all age groups up to fifty years. The menfolk in this age range tended to be employed in agriculture or the stone industry, and some of those men recorded as handloom weavers may have had employment outside the home from time to time.

By the 1861 census two mills were operating, and when the 1871 census was taken there were three. The data for both show increases in the total number of cotton operatives, this being concentrated among those below the age of thirty while the percentage of those in the higher age groups had dwindled. Though the censuses after 1851 do not distinguish between hand- and powerloom weavers, it is most likely that those in the younger age groups were working in the mills and those over thirty years old were continuing to use handlooms. Mill work attracted a large proportion of females, whose opportunities for work outside the home had hitherto been restricted to domestic service. Four mills were in operation by the 1881 census and, although the bulk of cotton operatives were still between the ages of ten and thirty, the larger proportion of people in the higher age groups reflected workers who, recruited in their youth in the early days of the mills, had stayed on over the years.

(For comparison with farm- and stoneworkers, see page 57.)

Although one might think of stone, agriculture and cotton industries as the major employers in the area, there were also many people who provided a service in shops, trades and public work. A common feature, too, was the employment of women, usually young and unmarried, in domestic service, most often on farms. A comparison of the relative sizes of these occupational groups in the village and in rural Alston has been made in the accompanying graphs.

The occupations listed as 'services' for 1851 are surprisingly numerous: grocer, greengrocer, butcher, baker, draper/tailor, dressmaker, mantua maker, clog, boot and shoe maker, innkeeper/beerseller, earthenware dealer, rag gatherer, washerwoman, charwoman, errand boy/girl, blacksmith, nailmaker, carpenter/joiner, plumber, glazier, painter, flagger, slater, wheelwright, coal man, saddler, cart driver, book-keeper/clerk, tanner, barber, doctor, school teacher, relieving officer, policeman, waterworks, letter carrier, lodging-house keeper, parson.

As the village expanded so did the variety of services offered. In 1881, in addition to those of 1851, there were: staymaker, cattle driver, ostler, vet, corn dealer, druggist, wood feller, sexton, clock and watch repairer, railway workers, hawker, land drainer, Prudential insurance agent, printer and stationer, inland revenue officer, gas workers, chimney sweep. (Foundry workers are included in this section, although they do not fit the criteria.)

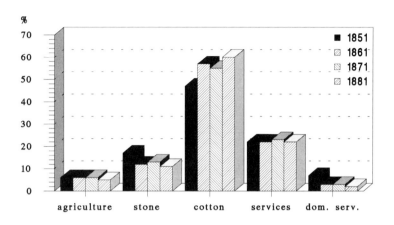

Longridge Village
Percentage Distribution of Workforce 1851–81

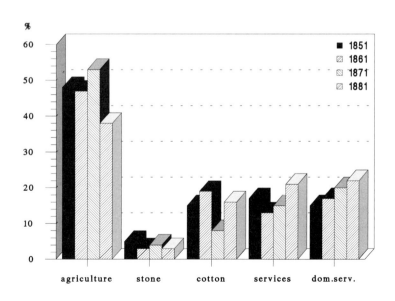

Alston (excluding Longridge village)
Percentage Distribution of Workforce 1851–81

Chapel Hill Junior Football Club, probably between 1905 and 1910. There were several local adult and junior teams in the village at that time. Someone was usually available to take photographs of the adult teams in kit, but not so for the juniors, and these enterprising lads, dressed in their best clothes, went off to Preston for a studio photo.

In August 1853 the usual holiday gala was held, but on this occasion it was joined by a group whose motives differed from the majority. The *Preston Pilot* reported,[14] '. . . During the afternoon a deputation from the operatives of the district, consisting of Mr Wm. White, Mr John Grampus and Mr A. Rasper, preceded by the fife and drum band, came into the village, and in the evening they advocated the "ten per cent movement" in able and eloquent speeches.'

There was considerable trouble in Lancashire mills at this time, the 'ten per cent movement' advocating agitation and strikes in its aim to secure a 10% rise in wages for mill operatives. After a strike in Stockport demands were met and later, to a great extent, in Blackburn, though Preston masters were reluctant to concede, stating that it was not a matter of wages, but of who were to be masters in the mills. The deputation mentioned above appears to have been attempting to involve the Longridge mill operatives in the movement, but there is no evidence that they were successful.

Twenty-five years later Longridge did not escape industrial trouble, as Smith records:[15]

Longridge was the scene of a disorder during the memorable lock-out of 1878. On May 16th, a rude effigy of Mr Henry Waring, Chairman of the Longridge Manufacturing Company, was burnt at the rear of King Street, amid yells and cries of a large but good humoured mob. About nine o'clock the same evening, an attempt was made to hustle Mr R. Smith, of Victoria Mill, but the police prevented it. My father, however, employed a large number of private watchers to guard his house, and I shall not forget the anxiety I felt as I lay awake at night, listening to the steady tramp of the 'special constables.' We were in fear, not so much of the Longridge people as of the Blackburn rioters, and so real was the fear that a troop of dragoons

Belmont Brass and Iron Foundry, which was run by a branch of the Bond family. It was situated off Inglewhite Road, on a site now occupied by a rest home. In the foreground of this photograph, to the left of centre, is Belmont Garage.

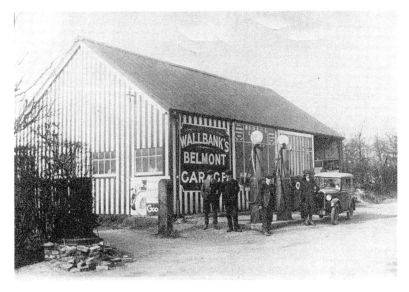

Belmont Garage in the 1930s.

was in readiness to march on Longridge from Preston.

A good deal of distress was experienced by the operatives, and relief was given by the Vicar and some of the employers of labour. Eventually, after a struggle lasting two months, the operatives submitted to the reduction of 10%.

In 1924 all the textile workers in Lancashire were on strike as their employers wanted to reduce wages. In this case it was the employers who lost their cause and after eight weeks normal work was resumed.

The Longridge Weavers' Association was formed sometime in the year 1878, though for some years it experienced great difficulties and made little headway against the marked hostility of the local employers. In a rural area the difficulties of organisation were great, but by dint of perseverance the association ultimately became firmly established. The Longridge District Association later wound up in 1964.

For one hundred years the mills were the principal employers in the village. At the height of their production there were over 2,300 looms in operation. The *Cotton Spinners & Manufacturers Directory* for 1904 lists them as follows:

George Whittle & Co. Stone Bridge Mill
560 looms
shirtings, cambrics, jacconettes and fancy goods.

Hayhurst & Marsden, Crampoaks Mill
6,400 spindles, 501 looms
cambrics, embroidery cloths, lenos, satins & umbrella cloths

Robert Smith Victoria Mill
690 looms
cambrics, jacconettes, twills, checks, lenos, fancy muslins, leno brocades.

Longridge Manufacturing Co. Ltd.
552 looms
cambrics, satteens and fancies
Joseph Johnson, manager. Christopher Holme, secretary.

In general the mill housing was of a very good standard and certainly far superior to those which gave the large mill towns such a bad name. Dickens may have based *Hard Times* on Preston, but he could not have applied that title to conditions in Longridge. Although clogs and shawls would have been the most common garments, their wearers were not living in slum conditions. Indeed all the mill houses remain and still provide adequate and comfortable accommodation.

Other industrial entrepreneurs recognised the advantages offered by the railway. A steam-operated bobbin mill was opened in Victoria Street, its main building still standing in the yard of Walter Carefoot & Sons. This mill was the successor to the water-powered bobbin mills on Cowley Brook near Knowle Green which had earlier supplied the handloom weavers.

Two brass & iron foundries were opened on the Inglewhite Road. The Poplar Foundry was established about 1870 by one of the sons of the then proprietor of Tweedys at Chipping. The trading name was Bond & Co. Around 1890 an association was made with a company from London by name of Davey & Co. Ltd. and the name of the foundry was changed to Bond Davey & Co., trading under this name until 1932 when Bond Davey

Ilston Lane Chapel 1774 RC
Church of Our Lady of St. Michael 1854 – 1890
Walla Field Chapel — Chrishley Congregational Private house
Kendle Green Congregational Chapel
Flattield church in private house
Bury Lane School – girls, boys in parts
1890 St. Paul's church Bury Lane

Dvorak Philip Rang BPO Octet Chchstra
Abril Symphonic Jarvi Chchs
Rybo Carl Christian Noras
Treasures of Baroque Open Dance Open Gde.
Bat Celeste S1, 202, 239 Guibal Teldec (Delph cottage)
White Bull, Dilworth
Spencers Arms, Longton Row (Dilworth Lane) – late century
Lee House, Thornley 1738 Prior building c 1830 RC chapel
St Wilfrid's 16 1869
Police station – Chapel Hill, No 2 Hylls/(High Ohm) Fell Brow (Chadhill)
Pitt St (Daly M)1880 – shield above door

Longridge

Parish church St Lawrence

White Bull Alston
White Bull Dilworth
Old School was church 1832 (now junior)
White house (Odd Fellows) Hothersall
Old Parsonage
Old farmhouse

Hawking Hall ? (Alston) 1608
Crumpax (Dilworth) 1596
Berry's Farm (Alston) (17)
Chapel Barn (   )
Old Dun Cow Rib 1616 Halfpenny Lane
Birkss, Thornley built 1616 front c 1780
Chingle Farm, Chingle Green

Tootle Heights Park

Flemings Square 1493
Club Row 1493
King St Houses c 1805
Handloom weavers cottages eg Fell Brow

Newton 1828 - 40 26 houses Handloom weavers; nailmakers; in - flaw sheds
Anthony's Also doctor's here, with date stone 1911
No 8 was a beerhouse
Cotton mills Whittles, Stone Bridge, Cornpoole Victoria Queens
Cotton workers houses Silver St, Chatham St, Mersey St.
Co-op Berry Lane 1880 Triangular
Grapes', Arms', Tootle Heights 1898 Plaque parliament
Red Lion Market Place 1795 datestone
Dog Inn 1713
Swarbrick Arms
Weavers Arms

Isham Degsay Grl
Schwanen Whitehead 24

Some of the workforce of Thornley Tile Works photographed in the early 1900s with field tiles which they have produced.

ran into financial trouble. The company was then reconstituted as Poplar Foundry Ltd., under the ownership of Mr Bert Duckworth of Ribbleton, who owned and ran the company until 1949 when it was acquired by the Blackburn family. It then traded under the name of Longridge Foundry Ltd. The foundry closed in 1971. The building was later acquired by Ryans, a building and construction company. The Bond Belmont Foundry was on the opposite side of the road and set well back from the road. This was demolished some years ago. Both foundries specialised in producing brass fittings for ships.

A footpath runs from opposite Belmont Garage, on Inglewhite Road, to Cockleach Lane Ends and walkers will notice that at each end the path is quite wide. Indeed, at one time this route was called Old Clay Lane and was a through cart road. The boundary between the townships of Whittingham and Thornley crosses this route. On the Thornley side of the boundary was Lord Derby's tile works, and it was here that clay that gave the lane its name was dug, and used in the kilns that were on the same site.

CHAPTER 11

The Village Grows

P RIOR to 1851, apart from two cottages, the only buildings to disturb the green fields on either side of Berry Lane were those associated with the railway, the largest of these being the Station Hotel, later called the Towneley Arms Hotel. It is noteworthy that in the 1851 census this hotel was considered to be outside the village of Longridge. This serves as a reminder that at that time the village consisted only of the houses stretching from Cut Thorn to the Duke William. Basically it was a linear village with a detached settlement at Newtown.

The census returns of 1841 to 1881 do make it possible to chart quite accurately the growth of the village during those years of expansion when hundreds of additional hands were required in the mills.

			Density per house
In 1841	1,006 people lived in	191 houses	5.3
In 1851	1,052 people lived in	206 houses	5.1
In 1861	1,462 people lived in	305 houses	4.8
In 1871	2,377 people lived in	531 houses	4.5
In 1881	2,975 people lived in	689 houses	4.3

Naturally one must ask the question, 'Where did all these people come from?' An analysis of birthplaces given in the census returns will provide much of this information, but it is not appropriate here to set out such detail. It is perhaps sufficient to say that people arrived from many distant parts, but a considerable number were attracted to the village from surrounding rural areas. No doubt the wages in the mill were better than those in agriculture and there was the opportunity for wives and children to find employment in the cotton industry also. In 1881 there were living in the village 148 people who were born in Goosnargh, 166 from Ribchester, ninety-six from Chipping and eighty-eight from Thornley. Bearing in mind the populations of those townships, the loss of so many inhabitants must have been sorely felt. These figures can be compared with a mere 183 persons from Preston. This represented a very small percentage of the population of that large town which, of course, had its own cotton industry.

Between 1851 and 1861 two mills were built and an additional ninety-nine

At one time it was quite usual to arrange one room of a house as a shop. This sweet shop was known as Mother Green's and was next to St Lawrence Church. The photograph was probably taken between 1905 and 1910.

These buildings were built by Joe Fletcher at the beginning of this century. Their architectural style is quite different from the rest of Berry Lane, or of Longridge, for that matter. The curved arches above the windows and the insertion of decorative terracotta tiles in the upper half make this corner quite distinctive. Originally, the telephone exchange was here, and was operated by one of Mr Mercer's daughters.

houses, a number of these being infilling between the Old Oak and Market Place. Completely new developments were in Pitt Street (Derby Road – thirteen houses) and Silver Street (sixteen houses), but only eleven houses had been built in Berry Lane.

The period between 1861 and 1871 saw the opening of a third mill and was the decade of greatest expansion, when the population rose by over 60% and the number of houses in the village by over 70%. It was at that time that the fields bordering Berry Lane disappeared under the construction of

The post office has occupied its present position for over 100 years.
Next door was the ironmonger's shop, run by Hedley Booth, which later became the Co-operative Society's greengrocery shop. Further to the right, across Irwell Street, was Foley's, the grocer. Inside, a system of overhead cables carried cylinders containing customers' money to a corner where Mrs Foley dispensed change, and kept a watchful eye on proceedings.

another sixty houses and shops, and at the same time the adjacent roads of Brewery Street, Dunderdale Street, Chapel Street, Mersey Street, Lune Street and Stanley Street were built. Twenty-five more houses were added in Pitt Street as well as five in George Street, seven in Mary Street and fifteen in Chatburn Road. Advertisements for the sale of building plots appeared in the newspapers. The following example from the *Preston Pilot* is dated March 1868:[1]

Longridge – To be Sold by Auction,
by Mr John Banks at the house of Mr Dunderdale, the Dog Inn,
on Wednesday the 18th of March:

Lot 1 All that newly erected Messuage or Dwelling House with appurtenances situated and fronting to Bury Lane, in Dilworth, and near the Longridge Railway Station and in the occupation of Mr Samuel Siddall.

Lot 2 All that other newly erected Messuage or Dwelling House with appurtenances situated and fronting to Bury Lane aforesaid and adjoining Lot 1 and occupied by Mrs Fletcher.

Lot 3 All that Plot of Building Land adjoining Lot 2 and having frontage of 46ft 10ins to Bury Lane and running backwards on the south side of and along a new street there intended to be called Severn Street.

There is space on the land for three Dwelling Houses of the class and description of Lots 1 & 2.

Lot 4 All that other Plot of Building Land adjoining Lot 3 and situate on the south side and having a frontage to Severn Street of 15ft 7ins and which plot is No. 4 on vendor's plan.

Lots 5 to 10 inclusive All those six other Plots of Building Land on the south side of Severn Street each of which plots has a frontage to Severn Street of 15ft 7ins and is in depth backwards 38ft.

Higher Road, Longridge.

Possibly the best-known feature on Higher Road was Harry Clegg's Cabin, on the corner of Green Lane. For many, many years this was a popular meeting place for the young people of the village.

Beyond is the terrace known as Cut Thorn. A change in roof line marks a change in building date: the three cottages at the far end are recorded on the 1837 Dilworth Tithe Award; the nearer houses were built between 1861 and 1871.

Lot 11 All that other Plot of Building Land situate behind Lot 1 and being on the north side of Mersey Street and having a frontage of 15ft 7ins and running in depth backwards 38ft.

Lots 12 to 17 inclusive All those six other Plots of Building Land on the north side of Mersey Street and running westward from Lot 11 each Plot having frontage to Mersey Street of 15ft 7ins and depth backwards of 38ft.

The building sites are choice, and have been so arranged to suit the view of persons wishing to erect on each Lot a comfortable House in the healthy locality of Longridge.

Plans may be seen – Mr John Banks, Strickland House.

Mr Thomas Smith, tailor and draper, Longridge.

A careful study of the above will enable the reader to pick out the dwellings which were actually built on the plots.

The fourth and last mill opened in 1874. Its requirement for hands kept up the momentum of house construction, and by 1881 the village had, more or less, taken on a shape which lasted until about 1945.

A rise in population of this magnitude must be accompanied by additional facilities or services to provide for the physical, mental and spiritual needs of the people. Many shops were included in the Berry Lane development whilst others appeared in Pitt Street to add to the existing ones in Fell Brow, Market Place, King Street and Langton Row (Dilworth Brow). Happily, in Derby Road, one 'Pitt Street' sign remains, attached to No. 82.

The first co-operative shop opened in Fell Brow in 1874, followed by another in Pitt Street in 1875, and a further branch opened in Lee Street in 1886.[2] After the opening of the first two shops business expanded so rapidly that land in Berry Lane was purchased and on it was built the society's central stores and hall, the most obvious and dominating of the new shops in Berry Lane. The corner stone was ceremonially laid in May 1879, and the fine new store opened in July 1880.[3] This original building is the part beneath the triangular pediment. It was not long before this new store became inadequate to cope with the increased trade and an extension was added in 1888. As well as shops, the society established a savings bank, reading room and library for its members. At that time the new store contained departments for drapery, furnishings, ironmongery, footwear, tailoring, butchery and bakery. No more building took place until 1933 when a further shop was built immediately below the central stores. This, in turn, was extended in the 1970s allowing the greengrocery shop, next to the post office, to close. For many years the co-operative movement flourished in Longridge and at one time there were six shops in various parts of the village. Times have changed, and during the 1980s increased competition led to the gradual closure of all the departments in the central store. Now only the food store remains, and shoppers no longer pop across the road to present their 'divi' slips, or collect prescriptions from the co-op chemist.

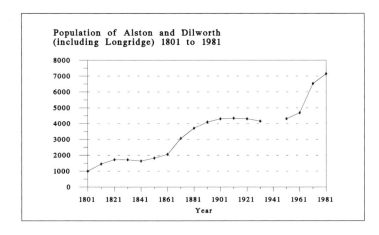

Population of Alston and Dilworth (including Longridge) 1801 to 1981

Prior to the mill era the inns were spread along the linear village from the Old Oak, passing the Duke William, the Wheatsheaf Inn, the Dog Inn, the White Bull to the Quarryman's Arms at Tootle Heights. The Towneley Arms was outside the village and was built to serve the newly-opened steam railway. Newtown also had a beerhouse, the Grey Horse. To these, after 1861, were added the Masons Arms, the Weavers Arms, the Swarbrick Arms (Empire Hotel), Red Lion, Spencers Arms and the Crown Hotel (replacing the Quarrymans Arms), the Durham Ox, Forrest Arms, Bull & Royal and the Stone Bridge Inn. However, Smith was pleased to state in 1888 that 'Drunkenness is almost unknown in Longridge'.[4]

He was not as complimentary about the inns themselves, describing them as dirty and squalid-looking drinking shops and, no doubt from first-hand experience, writes that[5]

> . . . none of them are better than ordinary third-rate Inns. With difficulty a dish of ham and eggs can be procured at the leading hostelries by giving long notice, whilst often bread and cheese are all you can procure. Such a state of things is simply a disgrace, not only to the owners and keepers of the Inns, but to those who patronise them.

Today, though, he would find them clean, warm, comfortable and inviting.

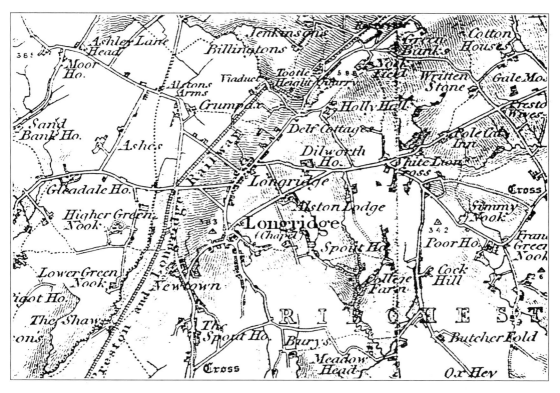

The rapid expansion of the village during the later part of the nineteenth century can best be appreciated by studying a map showing the area before many of the changes took place.

Although the map is dated 1852, the surveying for it must have taken place after 1836, but before 1842 when the first Alston reservoir was opened. The horse-drawn railway is clearly shown, passing under Stone Bridge, crossing Berry Lane and on to the Tootle Height Quarry. Newtown is shown, in more or less completed form, and also the Old Oak.

The linear aspect of the village, with detached groupings of cottages around the Chapel of St Lawrence and at Newtown, is well illustrated. At the lower end of Chapel Hill is Crow Trees Farm, demolished when the reservoir was constructed. Between The Spout House and Newtown is a farm with a

small plot of land stretching north; this was an orchard, on which Alston College was later built. At the north end of the village, opposite the end of Club Row, Strickland House (1798) can be seen and, further on, Square Fold and Cut Thorn. The houses at the north end of Cut Thorn were built much earlier than those at the south end of the terrace. Green Lane Farm, or Pearson's, is also shown, and notice the two farms, confusingly named The Spout House and Spout House. The latter is now called Alston Grange.

An ancient cross is marked at the junction of Preston Road and Pinfold Lane. Whether an actual cross was there at that time is doubtful, but the cross base is still in the field at that point. A clearly-defined cart road from here linked Preston Road with Hothersall Lane, but much of this has now been reduced to a footpath.

Alstons Arms is prominently marked

and bears the possessive 's', showing its ownership by Christopher Alston. To the right is a viaduct, where the railway crossed the track leading from Higher Road to Willows Farm. Originally there were two bridges in this area, but one was demolished when the playing field was made in the 1970s. The other still remains; the old farm road ran under the bridge whilst the railway above ran on to Lords Quarry. Access to Willows Farm is now from Chaigley Road.

Notice that there is only one Dilworth Reservoir. This, the present Dilworth Upper, was constructed in 1835. The 'lower' was not built until 1906. Opposite the reservoir a road leads to Jenkinsons. This was the original route to that farm and its neighbours before a new road (Chipping Road) was built across the marshy ground between the Alston Arms and the Derby Arms. The route of this old road remains as a splendid 'hollow-way'.

CHAPTER 12

Inns & Beerhouses

MENTION has already been made of Longridge's capacity for storing liquid, and the village also possessed a remarkable capacity for consuming liquid, particularly of the alcoholic variety. Inns and beerhouses opened their doors to the weary and thirsty every few yards, particularly on the old route up the fell road.

In order to appreciate their frequency one need only consider the temptation presented to the weary quarryman after his stint at the rock face on Tootle Height. As he emerged from the delph with aching limbs and parched throat he was confronted by the appropriately named Quarryman's Arms. This house was, and still is, adorned by an attractive date plaque of 1808 along with stonemason's tools (compasses, level and gavel or maul) and the builder's initials T.F., which probably refer to the father of the quarry owner, Thomas Fleming. It was not unusual for the quarry owners to attempt to extract from their workers the wages which they had previously paid them. As well as beerhouses they also ran 'tommy shops' which their workforce was obliged to use, as part of their pay was in the form of tokens which could only be spent at the shop. Tom Smith could see the obvious evil in this, but felt that he could partially excuse it by saying it was 'common practice'. The house ceased to have a licence between 1871 and 1881. After that it became Delph Cottages and later this century it catered for cyclists and ramblers before becoming a restaurant with a series of names – Cottage Café, The Berries, The Royal Sovereign, Mother of India, Pilgrims, Heathcote's. In its heyday in the nineteenth century it was used as the finishing post for an annual horse race which began at the Dog Inn. The race was part of the festivities of Longridge Guild Day, held on St Lawrence's Day during the second week in August. The first prize was a saddle.

The licence of the Quarryman's Arms was transferred to a new building close by. The Crown Hotel was built about 1871 and, unusually for that period, was built of brick, hence its unofficial name of Brick House or the Brick'n. Later, after it relinquished its licence, it became Crown Villa and then Beacon Flats. It has also been a youth hostel and a café.

Proceeding down the road the thirsty quarryman soon arrived at The White Bull, an inn which, in the past, played an important role in the affairs of the township of Dilworth, for it was here that the select vestry of Dilworth met

The datestone of the Quarryman's Arms.

Delph Cottages, Tootle Heights. These cottages were once the Quarryman's Arms. During the last thirty years they have been used as a restaurant, under various names.

In the 1920s the White Bull was the bus terminus. Notice the three-dimensional inn sign.

in the seventeenth century. Here the twelve or so representatives of the people dealt with problems relating to the poor, the highways, the church and the constable, and organised the collection of money to pay for these services. As was the case with many inns, the licencee was at one time a also farmer, and in 1851 Charles Foster is recorded in the census as 'Blacksmith & Innkeeper'. It was also the meeting place of the United Order of Odd-fellows, especially on guild day when there were annual processions, as well as being the venue for auctions of property, land, wood, etc.

Just around the corner in Langton Row (Dilworth Lane) was the Spencer's Arms, which can still be identified by the scar on the wall where the coat of arms was chiselled off. It was probably built by Spencer, the quarry owner, who lived at Rock House higher up the fell road. In 1861 it was run by John Banks, victualler and auctioneer, whose brother, George, who lived with him, was a quarry master. It was still in the Banks family in 1881 when William was described as 'Innkeeper & Farmer of 4 acres'.

No. 11 Market Place was The Red Lion Hotel, and the datestone of 1795 can still be seen. The Old Brotherly Sick Society assembled here each Whit Monday before processing, with other friendly societies, to St Lawrence Church and returning to an excellent dinner after which (in 1844) 'songs were sung and airs played by a band from Hurst Green'.[1] The Female Charitable Sick Society also used the Red Lion as a point of assembly for the procession.

A mere half-dozen steps took the drinker on to the Dog Inn. The present Dog was built in 1913 and replaced its predecessor which abutted the gable end of what is now the chemist's shop. These two buildings, although adjoining, were probably not built at the same time. It is difficult to determine whether the Market Place row was built on to the Old Dog Inn or the reverse. On Guild Day the Independent Order of Oddfellows assembled

The Old Dog Inn, Market Place. This was the predecessor of the present Dog Inn (1913), and was the meeting place for the Independent Order of Oddfellows.
Above the inn sign there is a vertical pole, and another can be seen a few doors to the left. This is on the Red Lion Inn, which was the meeting place for the Old Brotherly Society and the Female Charitable Sick Society.

Early open-topped, solid-tyred buses outside the new Dog Inn in the early 1920s. The position of the demolished Old Dog can be seen as an outline on the gable end of the adjoining building. Just appearing on the right is the elaborate front of the Swarbrick Arms, or Empire Hotel, as created by Joe Fletcher.

here and later returned for celebrations, as in 1844 when 'an excellent dinner was provided by Mr & Mrs Pickering, embracing both the delicacies and luxuries of the season'.[2] The inn must have been quite spacious, for in January 1852 the *Preston Pilot* reported: 'A party, to the number of about 180, were entertained to tea on Monday week in the large room of the Dog Inn by the respected landlady. After tea the company amused themselves with singing, dancing and other enjoyments, and altogether the evening passed over most agreeably'.

It was also the starting point for the horse race mentioned earlier. In the 1860s the publican was Robert Dunderdale, who owned land off Berry Lane which was eventually developed for housing and named Dunderdale Street.

A few steps further was The Swarbrick Arms, a beerhouse kept by Ellen Wilkinson and her daughter, Caroline, for over twenty years in the late nineteenth century. It had no cellar of its own, but used the cellar of the cottage next door. It was probably named after Richard Swarbrick, a farmer and butcher who was either living there or very close by in 1841 and later. He owned eight cottages in Newtown, two in Club Row and five in King Street. In the early years of this century it was acquired by Joe Fletcher, a local builder, who had a penchant for decoration and rebuilt the front façade, covering it with a riot of terracotta decoration. A large oval relief was placed over the door and little winged cherubic heads centrally placed over the lower windows, one of which bears a scar where the head was later broken off. The upper windows still retain much of their earlier splendour. Fletcher then changed the name to Empire Hotel. Since de-licensing it has served a variety of purposes, being a private house, home of the first Labour Club in Longridge, Y.M.C.A., shop, dentist's and dairy (not in that order).

The junction of Kestor Lane and Fell Brow, looking towards Market Place. The Wheatsheaf Inn (on the left) and the house to its right have long been demolished. Prefabricated buildings, used by Lancashire County Council Education Department, were erected on the site, and these in turn were demolished to make way for the present houses.

It took little effort to move on to The Weavers Arms, named in deference to the large number of handloom and powerloom weavers in the village. This beerhouse first appears in the 1861 census when Thomas Duckworth was 'Jerry Lord & Coal Dealer'. In 1871 it was run by John Edmondson whose parents had, over twenty-five years earlier, arrived in Longridge from Clapham, Yorkshire, and whose descendant became partner in the Kay & Edmondson quarrying firm. Originally the premises was quite small, but was enlarged when it was incorporated with a shop next door. It was the last 'home-brewed house' in Longridge and sold ale to the other public houses, a trade which ceased after the tragic death of the brewer who, it is reported, fell into a vat of beer and was drowned. There were stables behind for the horses which pulled the beer cart round the village.

Across the road, on the corner of Market Place and Kestor Lane, was The Wheatsheaf Inn, another of the older inns of Longridge. In the nineteenth century, the house next door but one to the Wheatsheaf was occupied by the Coup family, and prior to 1858 there was then a gap of thirty-one yards before the next house, occupied by Henry Shenty. This space was owned by David Nuttall, who had a handloom weaving factory where the cinema now is, and whose family had owned the adjacent Wheatsheaf Estate since 1764. In 1858 Nuttall sold the vacant plot, measuring thirty-one yards by thirteen yards, to James Marsden. Apparently, both John Coup and Henry Shenty had outbuildings on the gable ends of their houses, and actually on this plot: these buildings consisted of a petty, a bog hole and pig sty. It was agreed in the sale that these buildings should be demolished and replaced behind the houses of Coup and Shenty. In the thirty-one-yards space a terraced row (now numbered evenly from 32 to 42) was built, with a passageway at the south end to give right of way to the back of the six houses, and which runs under a bedroom of the present No. 42.

In his will[3] David Nuttall refers to: 'The Public House or Farm called the Wheatsheaf Inn or Tavern and the Cottage, Barn, Shippon, Stable, Outhouses and Gardens'. The Wheatsheaf is supposed to have lost its licence in the early years of this century for serving drinks and for gaming long after closing time. Its cellars were used as an air raid shelter during the 1939–45 war and the building demolished some twenty years later. It is of interest to note that in the early 1830s David Nuttall built Dilworth House on Dilworth Lane, later bought by Robert Smith, mill owner. There is evidence that during his occupation some alterations were made to the building.

The Mason's Arms, whose name reflected a local craft, was a beerhouse situated on Fell Brow and first recorded as such in the 1871 census. After a long period as a private house it was demolished in about 1970 when a bungalow was built on the site, this in turn being demolished in 1991 to make way for Alston View Nursing Home.

The persistent drinker would then require some effort to cover the next 200 yards or so to The Duke William. The original Duke stood directly in front of St Lawrence Church with which, along with some cottages, it shared an island of ground surrounded by roads. The inn was probably built in the mid 1700s and named after William, Duke of Cumberland, who concluded the Jacobite Rebellions with the total and bloody defeat of the forces of Bonnie Prince Charlie at Culloden in 1746. Depending which side one supported, this 'hero' was variously remembered as Sweet William, Stinking Billy or Butcher Cumberland. In the mid 1800s the Duke was the meeting place of the Roman Catholic Sick Club whose members, after the annual Whit Monday procession, enjoyed 'a capital dinner' provided by landlord, Jas. Pye. The demolition of the Duke in about 1880 made possible an extension of the burial ground and, strangely, provided one man with a most unusual record, for he was born in the Duke and later buried in the same spot. A new Duke was established across the road and in the 1920s underwent much alteration to its present form.

A bracing stroll down Chapel Hill leads to The Old Oak, strategically placed at the junction of Chapel Hill and Chipping Road (Preston Road), where it could atrract customers on either route. Its construction marked the completion of the Newtown housing project from which, no doubt, it hoped to derive its local clientele. It was built sometime between 1835, when the plot was purchased, and 1837, when it appears on the tithe map.

A few yards from the Old Oak and set in the middle of the main block of the Newtown hamlet was a beerhouse, The Grey Horse, affectionately referred to by locals as The Galloper. It was built, along with the rest of the cottages, between 1825 and 1835. Above the door was a relief figure of a horse. After the house ceased to have a licence the horse was removed and placed, by Joe Fletcher, on the façade of the Palace Cinema in Market Place, where it can still be seen. In 1871 John Fox Keighley was described as 'Beer Seller & Grocer'. The premises was, until recently, in use as a shop.

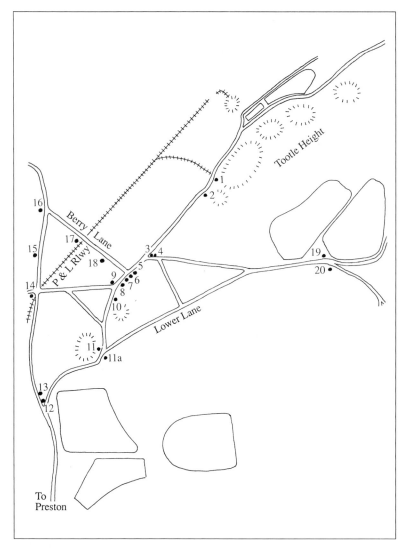

Longridge Inns and
Alehouses:

1   Quarryman's Arms
2   Crown Hotel
3   White Bull
4   Spencer's Arms
5   Red Lion
6   Dog Inn
7   Swarbrick Arms/Empire
    Hotel
8   Weaver's Arms
9   Wheatsheaf
10 Mason's Arms
11 Duke William
11a Former site of Duke
    William
12 Old Oak
13 Grey Horse
14 Stone Bridge Inn
15 Bull & Royal
16 Forrest's Arms
17 Towneley Arms/Station
    Hotel
18 Durham Ox
19 Corporation
    Arms/Black Bull
20 White Lion

In the above descriptions use has been made of the terms inn and beerhouse. The latter term usually applied to a house where only beer or ale was on sale, whereas at an inn spirits also were available, and many provided food and some accommodation.

All the public houses referred to above, with the exception of the last one, were on the fell road, that is Chapel Hill, Fell Brow, Market Place, King Street and Higher Road. They followed this route because that is where most of the houses in Longridge were situated before 1860 and it was the route along which many travellers passed. However, the coming of the railway resulted in far reaching changes in the village. After 1848, when steam locomotives were introduced, an increasing number of passengers arrived and departed by rail. At the level crossing, where the line crossed Berry Lane, the Railway Company built The Station Hotel, later to be renamed The Towneley Arms[4] which, positioned as it was at the railway terminus, was well placed to cater for passengers from a wide area who arrived by horse, trap, cart or coach. It had an extensive yard and stables and also acted as posting house.

The remainder of the inns were built with the houses which were constructed to cater for the increased population following the arrival of the cotton mills. In Berry Lane is The Durham Ox first mentioned in the 1871 census. On Derby Road or Pitt Street as it was called earlier are The Forrest Arms first recorded in the 1861 census, and The Bull & Royal, originally called The Bull and first recorded in the 1871 census. On the corner of Chatburn Road and Whittingham Road was The Stone Bridge Inn, originally owned by George Whittle who had the Stone Bridge Mill. Finding that it was too convenient for his workers to pop across the road for a drink, he made it into an off-licence, as it still remains today.

To the considerable number of inns in the village can be added several more which are or were within easy walking distance, but were principally intended to serve their own localities or the needs of travellers. The White Bull in Alston has always figured prominently in the affairs of the township in which it stands. It was the meeting place of the select vestry of Alston of which much has been written earlier. The inn has a very old foundation and the present building has a datestone of 1611 built into the south gable. This stone was probably re-positioned after an earlier reconstruction. It must be remembered that it is sited not only on the Preston-Longridge road, but also close to the junction with Alston Lane. This lane, as well as serving the many farms and cottages on or near to it, ran down to a ford over the River Ribble and was part of an old long-distance route stretching from as far afield as Rochdale to Garstang and beyond. Thus travellers would approach from that direction also.

On the opposite side of the village is The Alston Arms, at the junction of Inglewhite Road and Chipping Road. Despite its name it is not in Alston, but is actually in Whittingham. It derives its name from a previous owner, Christopher Alston who in 1848 hoped to sell it by the following notice in the *Preston Pilot*:[5]

Lot 1 The Fee simple and Inheritance of and in all that well-accustomed INN or PUBLIC HOUSE, known by the sign of the Alston's Arms situate in Whittingham, with the Brewhouse, Barn, Shippon, Stable, Gig house and other convenient Outbuildings, together with the several Closes of Arable, Meadow and Pasture Land, situate in Whittingham and Dilworth containing 28 acres now in the occupation of Christopher Alston, the owner. Also all that Cottage and Garden, situate in Whittingham, aforesaid, near to the last mentioned premises and now in the occupation of James Eccles, as tenant.

The above Inn and Premises are situated within half a mile from the north side of the village of Longridge, about a quarter of a mile from the Preston

& Longridge Railway Station there, and at the junction of the Turnpike Roads leading to Preston, Blackburn, Garstang and Chipping. The Buildings are very pleasantly situated, commodious and built of stone. The Land lies compact and convenient and has been thoroughly drained, and is now in an excellent state of cultivation.

A mile or so distant is The Derby Arms in Thornley, situated again at a road junction. In common with many very old inns it was also a farm, as can be seen from its architecture, and the present large dining room was originally the barn and shippon. It was on the Earl of Derby's estate and was previously known as Derby's Arms. It is inevitable that houses which cater for the general public will, from time to time, entertain customers with anti-social tendencies. The following account from the *Preston Pilot* of 1847 is a good example of this.[6] William Henry Slinger, thirty-seven, was charged with 'stealing at Thornley, Sept. 25th, one pair of boots, the property of Ellen Greenall'.

Mr Walmsley, for the prosecution, called Ellen Greenall, who said she was staying at the Derby's Arms public-house in Thornley on the 25th Sept. She saw the prisoner there on that day; he offered two pairs of boots and a pair of stays for sale. He left about three o'clock, when a pair of boots were missed, which belonged to her. They had been placed in a kitchen through which the prisoner passed twice. She had last seen them about two o'clock and next at the Dog Inn, in Longridge, a little after four o'clock. Elizabeth Greenall was next examined by Mr Walmsley: She said she was the landlady at the Derby's Arms in Thornley; he offered the boots for sale, but she told him she did not want any. She never offered him any boots. The prisoner, in his defence, said the witness had given him the boots in order to have a stronger pair in place of them.

A witness, named James Keighley, next proved to going after the prisoner to Longridge, and getting the pair of boots from him, which he afterwards gave to police constable 201, the officer at Longridge. The officer called confirmed the testimony, and Ellen Greenall re-called proved the boots produced belonged to her. This was the case.

The Chairman put the evidence to the jury, and they immediately returned a verdict of guilty, and the prisoner was sentenced to be imprisoned to hard labour for two calendar months.

Higher Birks in Thornley was an inn in the seventeenth century when the usual route from Longridge to Chipping passed that way. A short distance beyond the Dilworth Reservoirs, on the lower of the two roads, is the farm, High House. This was The Dog and Partridge, which ceased to be licensed between 1861 and 1871. Reference has been made earlier to The Black Bull Inn in Dilworth and the reason for its change of name to The Corporation Arms. Almost opposite was The White Lion Inn, now White Lion Farm, and on the Knowle Green road was the Pole Cat Inn. It must have ceased to be licensed before the 1841 census as it is then referred to as a farm only.

If walls could only talk those of the ancient inns of Longridge would have many tales to tell. Tales of the land, of fine harvests or of ruined crops, of wet summers or drought conditions, of sweated labour in the quarries, of life in the cotton mills, the bobbin mills and the foundries, of laughter and sadness, of petty crime and even murder. One could even talk of the strangest customer ever to arrive on the premises:[7]

A few days ago a gentleman of this town [Preston] having occasion to go as far as Longridge, hired a 'tit' for the purpose from Mr Harding, livery stable keeper. The animal was a thorough-bred one and considered quite a crack mare, and carried her rider safe and sound to the door of the public-house at Longridge. While stood there, however, some person touched her on her flank, with a stick or a whip, and she made a bolt through the door – the gentleman being literally scraped off by the lintel and the sides of the doorway. Not contented with having made an entree thus far, she walked up the stairs, passed the first landing, and ascended to a bedroom on the second floor, when seeing she could get no further, she turned round and came down again, as quietly as possible, and without anyone leading her. Of course the inmates were pretty considerably surprised to find that they had such a lodger to entertain.

CHAPTER 13

Meeting Spiritual Needs

IT was not only the Anglican community which increased with the growth in population caused by the construction of the cotton mills after 1850; other religious denominations, too, saw an urgent need to cater for their members in the village itself. Before this time most of their meetings had been held at various locations some distance from the village.

The Catholics

PRIOR to the Reformation everyone would be served by the Chapel of St Lawrence. After the changes instituted by Henry VIII the considerable Catholic community in this area resorted to meeting in such places as the private chapel of Hothersall Hall which was occupied by the staunchly Catholic Hothersall family.[1] During the late eighteenth century discriminatory laws against Catholics were eased, so places of worship could be built, but it was still felt necessary to adopt simple designs and to site them discreetly. This is well illustrated locally in Alston and Thornley.

A mission was founded in Alston in 1765 followed by a chapel in 1774.[2] This first Catholic church was constructed by converting the upper floor of a barn, and was entered by a flight of stairs on the outside of the building. It was on a site set well back from the Preston – Longridge road and down a small lane, a fact which led to its being known as Alston Lane Chapel or Church – a name by which its successor is still known today. This humble meeting place served the Catholic community until 1854 when the present Church of Our Lady and St Michael was built. The presbytery was added over twenty years later. The old chapel was then used as a school, and served as such until new premises were built in 1927.

An even earlier mission was founded at Lee House,[3] in Thornley, in 1738, although mass was probably said in the old farmhouse prior to that date. It is said that, at an earlier period, notice that mass was to be said was communicated locally by the hanging out of washing in a certain field. Once this signal had been observed word was quickly passed that a priest was due to arrive. This parish was founded by Thomas Eccles, a yeoman farmer of Lee House who, on his death, left land and farms in trust for the use of the

Alston Lane Chapel, 1765 (From Blundell's 'Old Catholic Lancashire'.)

St Wilfrid's Church during the construction of the steeple in the 1890s. (Photograph courtesy of Lancashire County Library.)

order of St Francis. It was thus that Franciscans served at Lee House until 1840. The present chapel and house were built by Fr Francis Trappes, the last of the Franciscans, who served between 1827 and 1840. There then followed a dispute with authority which led to the closure of the chapel for nineteen years. After its re-opening in 1859 it was administered by the Benedictines. With the establishment of the parish in Longridge this rather isolated church had to struggle along with a very limited number of parishioners. It can no longer be thought of as isolated as it is within easy reach of the many worshippers who arrive by car.

Even in 1850, when plans for the new Alston church were formulated, the future expansion of the nearby village of Longridge could not have been foreseen. However, after 1860 the Catholics of Longridge felt that they should have a place of worship actually in the village. Subscriptions began to be collected and soon a field fronting Pitt Street (Derby Road) was purchased. The foundation stone of a school-chapel[4] was laid in 1867 followed by the opening of the completed building in February 1869. In those early days the priest in charge had no presbytery, but rented a cottage nearby. The continuing growth of population necessitated a larger building and so work began on the present St Wilfrid's Church, which is built of local stone and was completed in 1886. It is said that there was such co-operation in the local community that many Protestants helped the Catholics to bring stone to the site. The steeple was added later in the 1890s. The former chapel became a school and continued as such until its demolition in the early 1980s. The church and its school are in Dilworth and are intended to serve the residents of that township. Lee House (St William of York) and St Wilfrid's Church are in Salford Diocese, while Alston Lane Church is in Lancaster Diocese.

The Nonconformists

Congregationalism

NONCONFORMITY has long been strong in the area. Indeed, its origins here in Longridge can be traced back to the mid seventeenth century, and are recorded in some detail in the centenary booklet of the Congregational church, from which much of the following information is derived.

In 1662 parliament passed the Act of Uniformity which enforced the use of the book of common prayer on all ministers and congregations. Over 1,500 clergy throughout the country refused to accede and were deprived of their livings or 'ejected', and this led to a surge of Nonconformity. Here in Longridge, Timothy Smith, the minister of St Lawrence Chapel, refused to comply with the Act and was duly 'ejected', and this brave and conscientious man is now regarded as being the first Nonconformist of Longridge: '. . .he did not conform, and yet preach'd frequently in the Chapel afterwards. For it being an obscure Place, with a small Salary, there was no great striving for it.'[5] Later his house in Longridge was licensed as a meeting place for Presbyterians. Timothy Smith died, 'very poor' in 1672.

Of the many branches of Nonconformity, that of Congregationalism was eventually established, not in the village of Longridge, but in nearby Knowle Green. In the late eighteenth and early nineteenth centuries several water-powered corn, spinning and bobbin mills were built on Cowley Brook, the associated cottages providing a population which was sufficient to justify the building of a church at Knowle Green in the early nineteenth century. (The 1841 National Census records 120 people living on the Dilworth side of Cowley Brook in the immediate vicinity of Knowle Green.) This was achieved by the efforts of William Hayhurst, who arrived from Blackburn in 1829 to work in a cotton mill.[6] He found that:

> The morals of the people of Knowl Green were at that time very low: drunkenness, prize-fighting, swearing and football matches being regularly practised on the Lord's Day. There was no chapel or school nearer than Ribchester or Longridge, those being distant from two to three miles, and the people were sunk in gross spiritual darkness, being without God and without hope in the world.

His outstanding work for Congregationalism at Knowle Green continued until his death in 1850.

The increasing use of steam power in mills, and especially the building of such power-operated mills in nearby Longridge, led to the closure of the Cowley Brook enterprises and to a lack of local employment at Knowle Green. Many people began to walk to Longridge, or indeed move house there, in order to find work. (The 1881 Census records only sixty-three people living on the Dilworth side of Cowley Brook.) The Rev. Giles Scott, minister at Knowle Green from 1859 wrote:[7]

Longridge is distant from Knowl Green about two and a half miles and had a population at that time of about three thousand souls, and only one Church and one Wesleyan Chapel. I consulted with my friends there, who still retained their membership with our church, and we decided to rent a room which was called 'The Tabernacle' and began services there. For four years I went every Thursday night and every Sunday night, receiving for my labours one pound a quarter, which, little as it may seem, was a decided advance on the payment of the trustees of Walker Fold, though they had £100 in hand. We received the aid of a gentlemen in Preston for Sunday services, and succeeded in time in gathering such a substantial congregation as to justify us in entertaining serious thoughts about building a new chapel. [Walker Fold Chapel is now a private house near the Craven Heifer in Chaigley.]

A leaflet issued in 1863 and bearing the following sentences was a most persuasive way of beginning the funding of a Congregational chapel and school in Longridge:[8]

At Longridge, a devoted minister of Christ, the Rev. Timothy Smith, was ejected from the Parish Church in 1662 because he could not with safe conscience subscribe to the Act of Uniformity. What more suitable memorial of that event than to erect a substantial place of worship in which the glorious truths and principles held by the 'noble confessor' of 1662 may be proclaimed and perpetuated from age to age.

The response was such that the cornerstone of the new chapel was laid on Good Friday, 1865. Later the chapel was visited by that critic of local churches and chapels, Hewitson, who commented:[9] 'Inside its appearance is particularly clean and minutely spruce. The seats are strong and no difficulty is experienced sitting in them. The pulpit is massive, of tasteful design, and is approached on each side by a flight of steps. The members of the choir sing well; their voices are good – good for Longridge.'

Accompanying the chapel was a day school, called the Longridge Training School, which was opened in 1866 and was the first alternative in the village to the Church of England schools. It was so successful that the foundation stone of a new school was laid in 1867. This was planned by the new minister, the Rev. William Booth, a man of many talents, as Hewitson recognised:[10]

. . . Mr Booth has considerable adaptability of character, and would be sharp at nearly everything. He understands cotton, book-keeping, architectural designing, parsoning and divers other things. He designed the schoolroom, a capacious and excellently arranged building at the rear of the chapel; he designed the new house, nearly opposite the chapel, in which he lives; he perhaps designed several other places for anything we can tell, and, as we told him the other day, may be called a very 'designing' man. For his ministerial services he receives about £120 a year, and out of this he can save money.

In 1901 a further extension was made and was named after the minister: The Archibald Memorial School. This latter building was demolished in 1990.

Methodism

LONGRIDGE first appeared on the Methodist circuit books in 1788.[11] The first meeting place was at a farmhouse near Knowle Green. About 1806 they moved to a room in Langton Row (Dilworth Brow), and later assembled in an upper room at the top of Berry Lane. Here a sunday school was started in addition to the preaching services. Soon this room proved too small and subscriptions were called for with the intention of providing a purpose-built chapel. These wishes came to fruition in 1836 when the Mount Zion Chapel was opened in Calfcote Lane, which contained seven pews, six open rail seats, four forms, a stove, a pulpit and a harmonium. (This building is now a house.) In the early 1880s it was decided to erect a larger chapel towards the top of Berry Lane. A plot of land was purchased in 1882 and the foundation stone laid two years later, and construction proceeded so swiftly that the opening of the new chapel was able to take place in October 1884. It was most appropriate that the first child to be baptised in the new chapel was born just the day before the official opening.

The Old Mount Zion Chapel, Calfcote Lane, 1836–84. The chapel closed when the Methodist Church was built in Berry Lane.
(Illustration courtesy of Christ Church, Longridge.)

Union

IN due course the Congregational church became the United Reformed church, but an even greater change took place in the late 1980s when a decision was made to unite with the Methodist church. The new Christ Church required only one of the two buildings and opted for the larger. The smaller Methodist church was sold in 1991 for commercial use, while the new Christ Church was re-opened after extensive renovation and modernisation.

The Anglicans

IT was mentioned earlier that in 1868 St Lawrence Chapel was elevated to parish church. The new status did not impress Hewitson who, in 1872, wrote in quite a scathing manner of the building:[12] 'The side walls are coldly prosaic and the chancel has a calm, whitewashed, railway-arch look, with one of the poorest and most unedifying windows that can be imagined'. Even Tom Smith described the church as a 'barn-like' building[13] and did not seem unduly disturbed when the 'unedifying' window blew in during a gale.[14] However, an interesting feature was two 'locomotive' pews at the front of the church,[15] which were on casters and could be wheeled to one side if more space was needed. Not all the pews were freely available to parishioners. For instance, in the 1840s an advertisement[16] for Dilworth House stated that the occupant would also acquire a 'front pew in the south gallery of Longridge Chapel'. It would appear that the local notables looked down on the proletariat who filled the ground floor, for Hewitson adds:[17] 'The church was well filled with a rural, fairly-dressed class of people below, and with a smarter and much more finished-off galaxy of individuals above'. Hewitson continues with a description of the pews:[18] 'Nearly all the pews on the ground floor are open, sloped at the back, narrow in the seat, and wretchedly bad to sit in. They are the strangest, the most lumbering, and uncivilised pews we have noticed during the whole of our rambles'. Tom Smith enjoyed the 'privilege' of a gallery pew, but writes:[19] 'Mr Hewitson has not overdrawn his picture at all as I know to my misery, many a long Sunday. And in the galleries the seats are worse than downstairs, as in the front pews you have no room for your legs'. Indeed, a church document of 1881 states that 'these pews are only 2 feet wide, so that no one can kneel or sit with comfort'.

From 1860 onwards houses, shops and services began to cover the fields which bordered Berry Lane. St Lawrence Church and its school then found themselves on the extreme edge of the village and far from the hub of the new activities. The school became overcrowded and so a new girls' school was built in Berry Lane in 1865, followed by Robert Smith's boys' school next to it in 1885. The infant school, built in memory of the Rev. F. Cave-Brown-Cave, opened in 1896.

However, the church building itself was the major problem for the Anglicans. Unlike the other denominations they already had a long-established place of worship in the village. As early as 1868 some parishioners felt that the church, because of its dilapidation and shortage of accommodation, was not worthy of the expanding village. It was also on the edge of the community and far from its midst. But what was to be done?

In 1873 the situation was considered so serious that a committee was formed to examine possible solutions. The vicar, by virtue of his office, was invited to occupy the chair, and the following statement, setting out the problems facing the parish, was issued:[20]

> For a long time past the necessity of providing additional church accommo-
> dation for Longridge has been deeply felt, and has occupied the earnest
> attention of many of the parishioners and property owners. During the last
> quarter of a century the population has increased threefold, and the inhabi-
> tants now number over three thousand, of whom two-thirds belong to the
> Church of England. But while this startling addition to the number of souls
> to be cared for has been going on the provision of clergy and church sittings
> has remained stationary. The vicar has to deal single handed with a flock
> which has grown out of all proportion to his power of reaching and influ-
> encing it, and the Old Parish Church is just what it was when the village was

but an insignificant hamlet. In fact, for more than two thousand professed church people, not concentrated within a manageable space, but scattered over an area of 4,326 sq. acres, there is but one pastor, and a church which, at the outside, offers accommodation only for 600 worshippers. Ample provision in the meantime has been made for the Roman Catholics and Dissenters.

In the course of succeeding meetings three ideas were put forward: to renovate and enlarge the church; to build a new church near the centre of the expanding village, and use the existing church as a mortuary chapel; to build a new church and form a new parish serving Dilworth and including adjacent parts of the parishes of Goosnargh and Chipping. Naturally, the parishioners were divided in their solution to the problem. Opposing the renovation and enlargement of St Lawrence was a very influential group led by Robert Smith, who favoured the building of a new church in the centre of the village. The vicar, the Rev. W.C. Bache, strongly disagreed with this solution as it would produce two parishes and split the village. Having a rival parish on his doorstep did not appeal to him at all. Without his consent such radical changes were not possible.

As meeting succeeded meeting discussions became more heated and, far from solving the problem, led to the resignation of the vicar as chairman. Eventually, in August 1875, the committee felt obliged to issue a very bitter statement:[21]

That the promoters have during the last two years made repeated efforts to obtain the requisite legal sanctions for the formation of a district for the proposed new Church.

That those efforts have on various pretexts been constantly opposed by the Vicar of Longridge, who has not hesitated to use any means in his power to obstruct the movement, and he has induced the Vicar of Goosnargh and the Patrons of Longridge and Goosnargh to support him before the Ecclesiastical Commissioners and the Bishop of Manchester in his opposition.

That in consequence of this opposition the Ecclesiastical Commissioners and the Bishop of Manchester withhold their assent to the project, and the promoters have no hope of bringing about a change in the attitude of those authorities.

The Committee have therefore come to the conclusion that their scheme must be abandoned, and therefore they abandon it accordingly.

The Committee willingly recognise that the defeat of their project is due to the action of the Vicar of Longridge, and they presume that in consequence of his success that Gentleman will accept the responsibility of himself providing for the Church extension, if the necessity for it exists, or of affirming that the present accommodation is sufficient.

A further statement added: 'So to the grief and disappointment of thousands, has ended the patient and praiseworthy effort of the leading Churchmen of Longridge to meet the growing spiritual necessities of their populous and extensive parish'. Two years later, in 1877, the vicar retired and a successor, the Rev. F.A. Cave-Brown-Cave, was appointed.

Shortly afterwards the Duke William Inn, which stood in front of the church, was demolished and the land on which it stood was purchased by the church. Some parishioners had donated money on condition that a new church was built on the plot, whereas others thought that it was intended for burials. (When originally built as a chapel-of-ease, no burial ground would be required as all burials took place at Ribchester.) Confusion reigned. There were also many other problems relating to burials and graves, and the vicar sought advice from many quarters. Some replies were frustratingly unhelpful, though strangely amusing as illustrations of English legal niceties. The vicar, therefore, called a meeting to discuss the matter, because, far from solving problems the acquisition of the new ground seemed to create more. That particular meeting was reported in the *Preston Herald* in January 1881 under the heading, 'The Burials Question'.[22]

The vicar said that he had been advised that any approach to lawyers would cost money, and he therefore contacted one of his friends, an eminent Queen's Counsel, hoping for free advice. His friend replied that barristers only gave opinions when instructed by solicitors. He could give the vicar his private views but, as these could not be made public, they were of little use. As the recent Burials Act had been drawn up by the government, the vicar decided to ask the home secretary for clarification. In reply Sir William Harcourt said that although parliament passed laws it was up to judges to interpret them. Such a situation, bordering on the ridiculous, brought much laughter from the meeting.

Another problem was the use of a beautiful pall which had been provided privately. As Dissenters (Nonconformists) were also buried at the parish church, should they be allowed use of the pall? This query had been put to the bishop. His lordship replied, 'I should hope that parishioners would have no objection to their being allowed the use of the pall if they requested it. I do not think they could claim it'. This also raised the question of the churchyard fence: if the Dissenters used the churchyard they should help with the cost of maintaining the fence. The report then referred to another problem facing the vicar:

One other matter he had to mention regarding graves, a matter which he was sorry to say would have to come before them shortly, though he hoped it would not be in a painful, but rather in a friendly way. The relatives of a person who was interred in the churchyard, a person who was very much repected, had computed for a double grave space, and on their own responsibility they had taken as much (at the smallest estimate) as would be required for three grave spaces. The result was that the sidestones were resting on the bodies interred on each side. Now this was not common fairness. People might be poor, but a poor man, aye, even a pauper, had as much right in God's house, and to have his bones laid in God's acre, as a

St Paul's Church. Although opened and consecrated in 1890, the church was not completed until the tower was added in 1937. It is a chapel-of-ease of the Parish Church of St Lawrence.

rich man, and a rich man had no right to place sidestones over the grave belonging to a neighbour. He had done all he could in a peaceful way to induce the parties concerned in this matter to remove the stones, and he hoped they would do so. The Vicar said it was not a matter of feeling, but one of common honesty and right. He would uphold the rights of the poor, as far as he could, in every possible way (hear, hear).

Replying to further questions on space for burials:

The Vicar stated that nearly 2,000 persons had been interred in the existing churchyard during the past 37 years, and if they looked at the croft facing the school they would see that it was large enough to hold 2,000 more. The number of funerals last year was 38, but the average number per annum was 42, so that the space would last them for 60 years without encroaching on the portion it was desired to reserve. He could only say that if Longridge Church was not rebuilt within 60 years it would be one of the interesting ruins of the neighbourhood (laughter).

After more heated discussion the vicar apologised after having criticized the Liberal government which had drawn up the Burials Bill. He agreed he should not have brought politics into the discussion. The meeting was then brought to a close.

Later, under the guidance of the Rev. F.A. Cave-Brown-Cave, further discussions were held, and eventually a possible solution was suggested. The vicar approved the building of a second church, but on condition that

138

the parish was not divided. Robert Smith immediately gave a plot of land off Berry Lane and also a generous donation. Fund-raising began in earnest, the cornerstones of St Paul's Church were laid in July 1886 and four years later the completed church was consecrated by the Bishop of Manchester. The tower was not added until 1937.

It had been decided that the small St Lawrence Church should be renovated as a mortuary chapel, but many of the parishioners felt a strong sentimental tie to the old building and a strong desire to use it, and began another collection aimed at its complete restoration. Their wishes were not denied and in 1900 the work was carried out. It was at that time that the box pews were dismantled and used to panel the walls. The vicar then found himself with one parish, but with two churches. In these circumstances St Paul's, although the larger building, was designated a chapel-of-ease. Not unnaturally the one congregation was divided in its loyalty towards the two churches, some favouring one, some the other. In order to accommodate the differing wishes of the parishioners a compromise solution was devised: services at the two churches alternated, and each church had its own choir, choirmaster and organist. This was not the most economical way to run a parish, nor the easiest for the vicar to cope with, but in such circumstances these materialistic considerations were not held to be paramount. Today, one hundred years later, the same system still applies.

CHAPTER 14

Alston College

SOON after leaving Longridge on the Preston road one passes the site of a nineteenth-century public school, though the site is no longer accessible because it lies beneath the bank of Alston Reservoir No. 2. The life of Alston College was short, but eminently successful. In its early days it was known as Alston Commercial Academy. The college was the brainchild of the Rev. Thomas Abbott Peters, M.A., of whom Tom Smith in his *History of Longridge* writes:[1] 'Born of humble parents at Preston, Mr Peters is in an eminent degree a self made man. In early manhood he started a night school in Alston, and becoming well known for his training abilities, he was soon enabled to build his first school, Alston College, in 1854. The venture proved a great success entirely through the principal's untiring energy and perseverance'.

This indeed must have been a remarkable man. The census of 1861 records that he was then twenty-six years old and was born at Brockholes. He must, therefore, have been born about 1835 and must have been about nineteen years old when he founded the College in 1854. One is left impressed by this achievement and also that he had, even earlier, engaged in night-school teaching. Even after establishing his school he continued with his evening classes, which, according to a report in the *Preston Pilot* in 1858, were very well received.[2]

> On Sunday evening last, Mr Peters' pupils and friends who attend his Sunday evening class and lectures, presented him with a large and valuable Bible, having marginal readings and selected parallel references, printed at length, and commentaries of Henry Scott, condensed by the Rev. John MacFarlane, L.L.D., richly bound in Morocco and gold, as a small token of esteem for his instructions.

Mr Peters built his academy on land which was part of the orchard of a farm which was positioned between the present College Villas and Spout Farm. On this plot the first buildings were erected, consisting of the main building, chapel and two schoolrooms. Later, as the College expanded, he bought a smaller adjacent plot and built on it a students' hall and swimming bath with gymnasium nearby. A more ambitious scheme followed in 1869 when the Rev. Peters entered into an agreement to buy Crow Trees Farm from its owner, Mr Edward Riddell of Cheeseburn Grange, Northumberland.[3] He borrowed the money from Riddell and repaid it with 4% interest over the next five years. In 1870 a small portion was sold to William Nuttall, who built there the two houses called College Villas.

Having acquired about sixteen acres of land adjoining the college buildings, Peters was able to expand again, this time eastwards, and built another students' hall, studies, bedrooms, classroom, masters' room, billiard room and principal's room. Several acres were converted into a recreation and cricket ground complete with pavilion and flag staff.[4]

The census of 1861, seven years after the foundation of the college, records that there were sixteen students in residence. To this number were added Thomas Peters (twenty-six years) and his wife Annie (twenty-four years) and a staff consisting of one assistant master, William Lund (eighteen years) of Ribchester, Elizabeth McNally (twenty-nine years) general servant born in Ireland, Mary Meadowcroft (fourteen years) kitchen maid and James Davies (fifteen years) page boy. The students' ages ranged from seventeen years down to five years, six coming from Preston and the remainder from Liverpool (two), Bury (two), Bacup, Salford, Birkenhead, Accrington, Whitehaven and Warbrick. Of the sixteen two were girls. It must be remembered that the above students were boarders. Day scholars from the immediate locality also attended the college, but their numbers are not known.

The number of students recorded in the census is curious when compared with that mentioned in an article in the *Preston Pilot* in July 1858:[5]

> Three years having elapsed on the 29th June, 1858, since the erection of Alston School, it was considered an appropriate day for celebrating the event by a grand festivity amongst the pupils. Mr Peters, the master, who is very popular, and highly esteemed, and who has received every encouragement since the commencement, arranged, early in the day, for a procession of the scholars, numbering 200, and preceded by the band of the Militia. The procession passed off splendidly, and in the evening the pupils partook of refreshments and dessert, after which 33 prizes were awarded to those who had distinguished themselves during the past half year. A great number of marks were also given for extra improvement and attention. – The five weeks' vacation of the pupils commenced the same day.

It seems highly unlikely that around 180 students would be day scholars, and one explanation might be that the census was held when the majority of students was on vacation.

The ten years between 1861 and 1871 saw a great expansion of the College. The Census of 1871 records 105 residents of whom eighty-eight were students. They appear to have been accommodated in three buildings: fifty-five people in one, thirty-seven in another and thirteen in the third. The headmaster and his wife were assisted by a secretary, an academic staff of seven masters: music, french, mathematics, classics (two), general (two), a cook, two butlers, a chambermaid, a page and a servant.

This contemporary drawing of Alston College was used as an advertisement. It does not appear to have been an exaggeration, for its form matches the features shown on a plan.

The eighty-eight students were all male, ranging in age from ten years to twenty-two years. The reputation of the college was clearly widely known, as its scholars were world-wide in origin: forty-one came from England, thirty-two from Ireland, four from Scotland, four from Australia, and one each from Wales, Jamaica, Malta, Sierra Leone, Nova Scotia, Barbados and Italy. An academic establishment of this magnitude would require considerable space for classrooms, dormitories, kitchen, dining hall and staff quarters, and a contemporary etching shows a magnificent array of buildings suitably befitting its excellent reputation. It is interesting to recall that at this time T. Abbott Peters was only thirty-six years old.

The students appear to have been typical of all boarding schools, as an article in the *Longridge News* (unknown date) states: '. . . the students, whom, it seems, included a large number of foreigners, were not beyond sliding down knotted sheets after lights-out to nip across the road to the Old Oak for a bottle of whiskey, for which they paid the sum of three shillings and sixpence'.

In 1873 Peters negotiated the purchase of the Hermitage Estate in Grimsargh from the Chadwicks, for which purpose he obtained a mortgage of £4,000 from the Preston Permanent Benefit Building Society. The total area of the estate was more than twenty-two acres. In 1879 he required more funds to develop the amenities of his second school, and so mortgaged his entire Alston College Estate to the Carlton Permanent Building Society. In 1881 the Carlton Society was dissolved and, exercising power of sale, conveyed the Alston College Estates to the Borough of Preston for £2,250.[6] An entry in Barrett's Directory for 1889 records that the principal was then the Rev. J. H. Astley. No doubt Peters was at the Hermitage, but no reference in the advertisement suggests a connection with the Grimsargh school.

The rapidly-increasing population of Preston was presenting the water-works company with problems and it was clear that further water-storage facilities would eventually be required. To this end the company purchased the land of the Alston College Estate from the borough, an action which led directly to the eventual closure of the college. Demolition of the college buildings was in progress in November 1892, for the *Preston Guardian* reported:

> On Wednesday, an accident of a serious character occurred at Alston College. The Preston Corporation are at present engaged in demolishing the former residence of the headmaster, and that morning, without any warning, a large wall caved in, partially burying three of the workmen beneath the debris. The names of the men were Dewhurst and Gardner, living at Alston, and Ogden, of Hothersall. Ogden had both legs broken, and the other two men received serious internal injuries. Medical aid was at once called, and the injured men removed home.

A new reservoir was not constructed immediately, for in 1886 the present No. 3 was deepened. However, droughts in 1887, 1888, and 1889 caused work to begin in 1894.[7] The college buildings as well as Crow Trees Farm had already been demolished and water first entered the new reservoir (present No. 2) in 1899. The only buildings to survive the flooding were those of College Villas which still remain opposite the Old Oak.

The *Longridge News* article quoted previously also states: 'A souvenir of the Alston College is to be found in the belfry of the parish church, for when the college buildings were demolished the bell which tolled the students to their studies was presented to the parish church, where even today it calls people to church services'. The clock which adorns St Lawrence Church also came from the college, and it is also said that doors and other items of woodwork found their way into the cottages of nearby Newtown. Thus ended the comparatively short life of Alston College.

It will be noticed that for eight years Peters owned both Alston College and the Hermitage. It is probable that during that time the Hermitage was employed as a preparatory school for the college, as the prospectus of the Hermitage states that it had 'Special Advantages for Junior Pupils'. In its early years the Grimsargh school was known as The Hermitage, but the name was changed to St John's College probably at the time of the construction of the college chapel in 1882.

The following is Tom Smith's account of the college (*c.*1888):[8]

> One of the few high class schools in the district is St John's College, Grimsargh, the old residence of the Chadwick family, then known as The Hermitage. The College is prettily situated a little way from the high road to Preston, and close to Grimsargh Station. The school is fitted up with the most modern improvements, including airy and pleasant classrooms, a large swimming bath and gymnasium, besides cricket and football fields of nine acres in extent. There is also a beautiful chapel attached to the school, which

is licensed by the Bishop. We do not suppose that in any school in England better provision is made for the bodily comforts of the boys than at St John's College – a matter, though of such vital importance to growing youths, which is often neglected. *Mens sana in corpore sano* is evidently the motto of the Rev. T. Abbott Peters, M.A., the respected Principal, and Mrs Peters. The successes attained by the pupils at the various Universities, the Army and Civil Service, prove conclusively that every attention is paid by the masters of the school to developing the mental faculties of the students. A list of these successes during the last few years would fill many pages of this book. A striking proof of the fame which the college has attained is afforded by the number of pupils, which is now upwards of 100. We may add that the sanitary condition of the school is excellent.

It seems likely that Peters retired in the latter years of the century, for an entry in the Longridge church magazine for October 1901 states:

Harvest Thanksgiving Services will be held in S. Paul's Church, on Sunday, October 13th . . . In the evening the sermon will be preached by the Rev. H.G. Barnacle, M.A., Principal of S. John's College, Grimsargh.

Despite its excellent record, this school closed soon after the turn of the century. Rumour has it that students were involved in a tragic swimming accident on the River Ribble which resulted in a loss of confidence in the establishment.

It is perhaps sad that no trace remains of Alston College, but part of St John's still survives off Elston Lane. For many years it was a restaurant under its former name, The Hermitage. The chapel has been demolished.

CHAPTER 15

Public Services

Nineteenth-Century Policemen

THE census of 1851 records a police office on Chapel Hill, occupied by twenty-five-year-old police constable William Durham and his wife, Catherine (both born in Ireland) and their two children. There are two stations recorded in the census of 1861, one at No. 2 High Street (Higher Road), and the other at the bottom of Fell Brow (now Chapel Hill). In later years there is no further reference to the High Street station, but the one in Fell Brow/Chapel Hill continued in use until the present one was built in Pitt Street (Derby Road) in 1880. Above the door can be seen the remains of the shield which carried the constabulary coat of arms.

P.C. Durham's (Derham's) work was not without incident, as is well illustrated by this account in the *Preston Pilot* in February 1852:[1]

On Tuesday, Robert Earnshaw, James Whalley, Thomas Heskin, Thomas Martin, and James Parson, of Longridge, were charged with having been riotous and disorderly, and with assaulting Wm. Derham, of the county constabulary, under the following circumstances: It appeared that about one o'clock on the morning of the 1st inst., about nine or ten persons who had been drinking at the Dog Inn, assembled opposite the door of the house, and as they were very noisy the constable went up to them and requested them to go home, but was answered with a shower of stones. The constable retreated into a corner of the building, but as the crowd continued to throw more stones at him he ran towards them to see who they were, when Robert Earnshaw struck him a blow in the mouth, and his hat was knocked off. A man named Regan, who was with the constable at the time, came to his assistance, and Earnshaw was taken into custody. On the way to the station, Earnshaw was very violent, and as they met Thomas Heskin, the constable requested his assistance, which was refused. They afterwards met Whalley, who gave his assistance when required, but after going with them a short distance he suddenly let go his hold and shouted to the mob who were still following, 'Now lads,' while Earnshaw cried, 'Come on lads, be men.' Another rush was made at the constable, who was knocked to the ground insensible by a blow on the head with a stone, and the prisoner was rescued.

Regan kept back the crowd off Derham for some time, and the latter recovering consciousness got up, but was twice knocked down and brutally kicked by several of the prisoners. Regan being also knocked down the crowd made off, and Derham was assisted home by Regan, having sustained very serious injuries. The prisoners were afterwards apprehended, and it being proved that they were all participators in the affray they were committed for trial at the sessions.

At that time there was only one police constable in Longridge and it would appear from other reports that he was assisted, on occasions, by members of the general public. There was no way in which he could quickly summon police reinforcements. There was no wireless, no telephone, not even a bike. The quickest method of getting a message to Preston was by horse. In any case, by the time a posse of police could arrive incidents such as the above would be over.

Two years earlier, at the beginning of November 1849, P.C. Derham was involved with a strange case which must have been a talking point in the village for months. It was reported thus in the *Preston Pilot*:[2]

This quiet and retired village was thrown into a state of considerable excitement on Thursday night by a report of the attempted murder of a female servant at the house of the Rev. C.R. Bache, of Alston, by firing at her through a window. As far as we have been able to ascertain the particulars of this occurrence they are as follow. Between seven and eight o'clock on Thursday evening, county police officer (368) Derham, who was passing up the road in Longridge, heard the report of a gun, and thinking this to be something strange at that hour of the night, he went in the direction from which the noise proceeded, and having gone for a short distance he ascertained that a young woman named Isabella Taylor, a servant with the Rev. C.R. Bache, had been fired at through one of the windows of the house. The young woman said that she was in the pantry when a gun was fired at her through a window and she was wounded in the head and face. On being questioned, the young woman said she suspected a labouring man named James Walmsley, who had been employed about the premises for the last six months. The policeman went to Walmsley's house about half past twelve yesterday morning and knocked at the door for admission. Walmsley appeared to be in bed, but he got up and came downstairs to the door and opened it for Derham, who went in and immediately charged him with firing a gun with intent to murder Isabella Taylor. Walmsley said he was entirely innocent and knew nothing about it. Derham then searched the house and found two guns loaded, and on examining the prisoner he found on him a quantity of shot and percussion caps. Derham then took him into custody, and locked him up. Immediately after the occurrence, surgical aid was obtained for the young woman, and the professional gentleman who was called in said she was severely hurt. On examining her head and face he found that about thirty shots had penetrated there, and in a door near which she stood there were at least a hundred more. We have not heard any motive assigned which could lead Walmsley to the commission of this horrible crime. No doubt the affair will undergo a thorough investigation, as the prisoner will be brought before the magistrates at the Town Hall this day.

The following week a further short report appeared:[3]

County Petty Sessions at the Town Hall
(Summary of additional information)
Certificate from Mr Glassbrook, surgeon, stating that Taylor was not sufficiently recovered to give evidence. P.C. Derham said she was exceedingly shy in giving information at the first, but ultimately said she suspected Walmsley, as she was in the family way by him, and had had some conversation with him that morning respecting it. The prisoner was a married man with two children and kept a small farm about three miles from Longridge and had borne a good character.

A week later there was more information published:[4]

(Further summary of resumed hearing)
Although speaking with difficulty because of her injury, Taylor, seated, gave evidence. She said that when the Bache family were away Walmsley was asked to stay overnight at the house for security reasons. On one such occasion when she was sitting sewing he pulled her on to his knee and held her tight and then sexually assaulted her. There was much evidence given by several people as to the whereabouts of Walmsley on the day and evening of the crime. He was committed to the Assizes at Lancaster Castle.

The case was eventually heard at the Liverpool assizes in March 1850.[5] The prosecution pointed out that Walmsley had both the motive and the opportunity for the crime. Also the lead shot found at the scene matched some of that found in the pocket of the accused. In his defence Walmsley said that at the time of the crime he was returning to his home (Bradley Lee) in Hothersall after attending a sale at Carwood House. Unfortunately he could not produce any witness to confirm his movements after leaving the sale. The defence lawyer also revealed that Walmsley was a churchwarden of Ribchester church:

Mr Overend, for the prisoner, addressed the jury in a most powerful and effective speech, contending, that although there might be strong grounds of suspicion against his client, no direct proof of guilt could be maintained.

His Lordship, in his summing up, observed that it was a matter of very serious consideration for the jury; he recollected many years ago that the proof brought against a man on trial for a similar offence was that three kinds of shot were found in the prisoner's house and three in the wound. Mr Dixon, the surgeon, giving evidence that the shot extracted from the face of the girl accorded with what was found in the gun of the prisoner. This was no circumstance against the prisoner; however it remained for the jury to decide.

After a consultation of a few minutes, the jury returned a verdict of not guilty, and his lordship immediately ordered the prisoner's discharge.
The last report on the incident appeared in May 1850:[6]

> An order in bastardy was obtained in the county petty sessions in the case of Isabella Taylor v. Robert Walmsley, the parties concerned in the trial for the mysterious attempt at murder which recently took place at Longridge. Mr Segar, barrister, appeared on behalf of Taylor, and Mr Ascroft for Walmsley. After a short consultation, an order was made for 1s. 6d. per week and expenses.

William Derham must have carried out his duties to the satisfaction of his superiors for, in 1855, he was promoted to sergeant, but as a result of the promotion he left Longridge. However his services to the local community were recognised when a presentation was held in October of that year.[7]

> On Monday evening, a meeting was held in the Mechanics' Institution, Longridge, for the purpose of presenting Sergeant William Derham, of the county constabulary, with a testimonial of the appreciation of his services by the inhabitants of Longridge. The Rev. W.C. Bache, Messrs W. Marsden, cotton spinner, H.B. Jones, Gledale-house, and several other respectable inhabitants of Longridge and its immediate neighbourhood were present on the occasion. The Rev. W.C. Bache, after an appropriate address, presented the testimonial, which consisted of a large rosewood writing desk, handsomely bound and inlaid with brass, and which bore the following inscription: 'Presented to Sergeant William Derham, by a few of the inhabitants of

The present police station in Derby Road was built in 1880, at which time it was well-manned by five officers.

Longridge, in testimony of the faithful and diligent manner in which he has performed his duties as police constable in that place. – A.D. 1855'

Sergeant Derham returned thanks for the testimonial in a neat speech. – The value of the writing desk is eight guineas.

Longridge folk seem to have appreciated their previous constable also for in 1845 it was reported:[8]

Testimonial of Respect – Longridge On Saturday last, Mr John Gardner, late Police Constable of the county constabulary at Longridge, on the occasion of leaving the force was presented with a purse of gold by the inhabitants of Longridge and the neighbourhood. A subscription had been got up for this purpose, and was received by Mr Henry Parkinson, yeoman, Longridge, Mr Whittle, Manufacturer, and Mr John Seed, and the inhabitants, desirous of showing their sense of the services of this officer, came liberally forward and the purse was presented to him as above stated. Mr Gardner very feelingly acknowledged the munificent gift, and assured the deputation he should never forget the kindness of the inhabitants of the village and neighbourhood.

The huge house-building programmes in the 1860s and 70s required an influx of tradesmen, some of whom seem to have been unsatisfactory in their conduct, for the 1871 census records three prisoners in the station cell. All were bricklayers – one each from Dublin, Liverpool and Preston.

Fire

COPING with outbreaks of fire in domestic or industrial premises is a problem that is ever present, though an efficient fire sevice does help allay some of our fears. Longridge has its own modern fire station, fire appliance and staff to supplement the full-time County Fire Brigade.

Nos. 43 & 45 Berry Lane are between the Towneley Gardens and Towneley Road and were built prior to 1889 possibly by Ellis Wilkinson, proprietor of a mineral water firm at No. 43. The mineral waters were in thick green glass bottles with a 'glass alley' in the neck. Wide doors provided the entrance for the lorries, both horse-drawn and motorised. In the late 1920s part of it was used as a laundry. The large entrance in Berry Lane was the way into a mini-market for greengrocery and fish. Later the rear of the building, which was formerly the laundry, was taken over by Mr Lawrence Bond, the maker of the three-wheeled Bond Minicar. It was thus occupied for quite a time until the firm expanded and moved to larger premises in Ribbleton Lane, Preston.

In 1939 the building was taken over by the Auxiliary Fire Brigade to house the local fire engine and telephone switchboard, a use which continued until the building of the new fire station in Whittingham Road in 1967.

Prior to the introduction of motorised fire appliances and speedy communication through the emergency telephone service, dealing with fires was a very chancy business and is well illustrated by this newspaper account of a fire in Longridge in December 1848:[9]

On Monday morning the warehouse belonging to Mr Whittle, manufacturer, at Longridge, was partially destroyed by fire. There were two men and two boys at work in an upper storey of the building at about a quarter before seven in the morning, when they perceived a smell of burning in the room. They immediately proceeded into the warehouse below, which they found in flames. An alarm was then given, the neighbours were aroused, and every assistance afforded, and a lad was dispatched on horseback to Preston for a fire engine. Water was obtained from the cisterns and water buckets. An attempt was made to re-enter the warehouse by a front window, in order to act more effectually upon the fire, but the dense smoke prevented this. An entrance was eventually gained from the back by Mr Whittle, and water being quickly supplied, the fire was considerably reduced. The messenger who was dispatched to Preston arrived here about a quarter before eight, and a body of firemen being collected, Mr Graham, the efficient superintendent of the fire brigade, started with one of the engines and four horses for the spot. When they had proceeded a couple of miles, a second messenger met them with the intelligence that their services were not required, but as they had gone so far, Mr Graham considered it advisable to go forward, but when they arrived at Longridge the fire was completely extinguished. The warehouse was completely gutted, but the fire did not extend further. Great praise is due for the active exertions of the neighbours, and particularly to the females, who were actively engaged in carrying water in cans which they brought from their own houses. Mr Fleming considerately sent all his men from the delf, which is at a short distance, and they afforded very material aid. The fire is supposed to have originated in consequence of a lad whose duty it was to kindle the fires, having dropped the snuff of his candle into a skip of paper. The damage is estimated at £500, and we believe the property is insured in the Sun Office. We are glad to learn that the business at the works will be carried on as usual, and that the disaster will not throw any hands out of employ.

The Gas Works

ON 26 October 1867 the following report appeared in the *Preston Pilot*:[10]

The works for supplying this village with gas, which have been in course of construction for some time, are now so far advanced that it is hoped they will be completed in the course of another month. The mains are all laid, and the pipes have been connected with meters in such of the shops and houses as the occupiers have notified their intention of being consumers.

There is no doubt that gas would have been ready ere this, but several
accidents in the construction of the gasometer, etc., have somewhat retarded
the work.

It was followed up on the 21 December with:[11]

The Gas Works at Longridge have so far progressed that gas was lighted for
the first time on Sunday evening last, and on Monday evening the directors
and promoters of the movement celebrated the occasion by a supper at the
Dog Inn.' And so gas came to Longridge.

For a number of years the spread of a gas supply to the public was
hampered by its high cost compared with paraffin oil, which was in common
use for house lighting. At a meeting of the gas company[12] in 1881 the
chairman forecast a rise in the price of oil and thought that the Longridge
public 'ought to be thankful for what the company had done.' The company
was disappointed by the lack of progress in street lighting:

The company had been in existence more than 13 years and one solitary
street lamp was all they had in the place. This lamp was erected as a
'schoolmaster' to teach the people the benefit of light, but he was sorry to
say it had failed to accomplish the task as yet. A well lighted village would
benefit them morally as well as physically. There was a prospect now of the
thing being done, and perhaps by another year they would see their streets
lit up with gas.

In 1883 the Local Board borrowed £150 from the Order of the Druids to
help pay for the installation of some gas lamps, and Thomas Attwood was
appointed lamplighter at 10s. 0d. per week. This venture had its problems, for in the following February playful winds blew out many of the
lamps. Some alterations were made to some of the lamps, which were
then sited in draughty places to test them. From this time the number of
lamps installed increased so that more lamplighters were employed.
Eventually they became unhappy with their increasing workload and
petitioned the Local Board:[13]

The Clerk read a petition from the lamp-lighters asking for a small advance
in their wages. Their work had increased, and they thought their wages
should be again considered. – The matter was considered by the Board, and
it was resolved to increase their wages by allowing them to clean the lamps
in the Board's time instead of their own, as heretofore.

The streets continued to be lighted by gas until 1950–51 when conversion
to electricity took place.

The entrance to the gas works from Pitt Street (Derby Road) was via the
narrow Gas Street. This was originally cobbled and over the years horses

and carts taking coal to the works had produced deep ruts. In 1931 the manager asked Walter Carefoot if he would concrete part of the roadway. Walter recalls that at that time he had recently bought a concrete mixer, the first in Longridge, and used it for this job. The mixer was quite a novelty and many folk hampered his work by coming along just to see this new machine. Eventually two tracks were concreted for the cart wheels, whilst the cobbles were left in the middle to provide grip for the horses.

Probably the best known incident concerning the gas works was the tragic accident which occurred in September 1905 when a boiler explosion killed two men. The *Preston Herald* of 30 September 1905 reported:[14]

BOILER EXPLODES
Fragments Blown over Houses
Two Men Killed and One Injured

Not for many years has there been such a terrible disaster in the township of Longridge as that which took place on Thursday morning.

A loud explosion, which was heard for miles around, occurred just before nine o'clock, appearing to come from the direction of the gas works, situate in Pitt Street. The residents of the village were alarmed and people flocked from all directions into Pitt Street and from there to the gas works yard.

It was seen that the large stone wall, formerly behind the boiler, had been carried bodily away by the boiler, which had ploughed up the field behind for a distance of 60 feet.

The remnants of an adjoining building and the stones from the wall were scattered all over the field. The former was used for the manufacture of sulphate of ammonia and was partially demolished. The forepart of the boiler was blown against the holder which stood nearby, making a large hole. This released the gas and the tank sank rapidly, whilst the pillars supporting the latter had not escaped the violence of the explosion. Had the boiler been driven any other way than in the direction of the field the consequences might have been more terrrible, for the works are nearly surrounded by houses.

One piece of boiler was blown right over two streets of houses, carrying away in its flight the roof of St Wilfrid's Men's Club, and falling into the grounds of the Roman Catholic Church.

It was at once apparent that loss of life must have resulted. The length of the boiler was about 20 feet, and its use was to provide steam for the making of sulphate of ammonia. It is surmised that the stoker, named William Bamber, aged 41, was attending to his duties when the explosion happened. Two other workmen named John Woodward and a man named Bland were in the retort house at the time and rushed out. They saw Mr Lancaster, the manager, at the other side of the large gas holder in the act of falling.

Woodward ran to his assistance, he being unconscious and having a large cut on his face. His clothes were wet. The large tank rests in some water and, it is thought, Mr Lancaster must have been thrown into this, being near the boiler at the time.

Scenes at the gas works after the tragic explosion in September 1905.

After the manager had been assisted into his house, which adjoins the works, a search was made for Bamber, the stoker. Woodward's search about the premises was futile, but on getting a hook and dragging it through the water in the holder the body of the dead stoker, badly burnt, was found, having apparently been thrown by the violence of the explosion against the tank and dropped into the water.

It was then remembered that a plumber and painter employed at the gas works, named John Ormerod, aged 39, must have been about the gas works, but frequently worked away in various parts of the district, but it was ascertained that he had been working at the gas works that morning. His body was also taken from the tank and it presented a shocking appearance.

The tragedy was compounded by the number of children left fatherless: Mr Bamber of 33 Pitt Street had nine children, Mr Ormerod of 47 Pitt Street had six children.

Conclusion

Continuing Change

THE emphasis of this story of Longridge lies in the pre-twentieth-century period. It has dealt in some detail with what was probably the most significant phase in the growth of the community, that is the years from 1850 to 1880 when the whole shape of the village was transformed and its linear layout was lost forever. It was those years of expansion which provided the basis for local employment for the next fifty years.

The second half of this century has seen a radical change in employment patterns. Gone are the industries which provided mass employment in the village itself. Now there tends to be a proliferation of smaller units such as civil engineering, light industry, transport, dairies, etc., along with a large variety of enterprises providing services specifically for householders.

Increased use of motor cars allowed residents to seek employment outside the confines of the village. The motorway network allows relatively easy access not only to nearby towns, but to cities such as Manchester and beyond. This mobility also encouraged an influx of those seeking an environment which had the advantage of a rural outlook along with urban shopping facilities. The last thirty years have seen the stone-built heart of Longridge gradually surrounded by an ever-increasing number of modern brick dwellings, and this, in turn, has led to an expansion of services required by this new community. Longridge now enjoys the status of a town, but has to solve or endure many problems such as traffic, car parking, and litter, as well as the provision of leisure facilities for its ever-growing population.

The aim of this book does not allow for a detailed analysis of the many facets of post-1950 Longridge, but it is hoped that it will have helped the reader to understand how the present stage has been reached.

Notes on the text

Chapter 1: Introduction

1   Dom. F. O. Blundell, *Old Catholic Lancashire*, Vol.1 (1925) p. 173; Ekwall, *Place Names of Lancashire*, p. 140 suggests a date of 1521.
2   W. J. Varley, 'The Bleasdale Circle', *The Antiquaries Journal*, Vol.18 (1938)
3   Rev J. R. Luck, 'An Account of the Opening of a Large Tumulus near Stonyhurst, Lancashire', *Transactions of the Lancashire & Cheshire Antiquarian Society*, Vol.12 (1894)
4   Harris Museum, Preston
5   Harris Museum, Preston
6   T. Hinde, ed., *The Domesday Book, England's Heritage Then and Now*, (1985), p. 151
7   T. Smith, *History of Longridge*, (1888), p. 22
8   T. Hinde, *op. cit.*, p. 155
9   *Ibid.* p. 155
10 T. Smith, *op. cit.*, p. 2
11 *Ibid.* p. 2
12 *Ibid.* p. viii
13 *Ibid.*, chapter 1

Chapter 2: The Chapel and its Village

1   T. Smith, *History of Longridge*, p. viii
2   A. Hewitson, *Our Country Churches and Chapels*,(1872) p. 94
3   L.R.O., QSP 451/2 (1676)
4   T. Smith, *op. cit.*, p. 50
5   L.R.O., The Alston Book, PR872
6   L.R.O., PR872, *Op. cit.*

7   T. Smith, *op. cit.*, p. 53
8   L.R.O., PR872, *Op. cit.*
9   T. Smith, *op. cit.*, p. 57
10 T. Smith, *op. cit.*, p. 36
11 L.R.O., PR872 (1784), *op. cit.*
12 Document in Longridge Parish Chest
13 *Preston Pilot*, 26 May 1838
14 T. Smith, *op. cit.*, p. 42
15 *Preston Pilot*, 1 June 1844
16 L.R.O., Transcriptions of Ribchester Parish Registers, (1906)
17 L.R.O., QSP 1346/1 (1732)

Chapter 3: Some Interesting Properties

1   T. Smith, *History of Longridge*, p. 137

Chapter 4: Local Government before 1900

1   L.R.O., The Alston Book, PR872
2   Charity Commission Report on Charities in the Parish of Ribchester, 7 June 1898
3   *Ibid.*
4   L.R.O. PR872, *Op. cit.*
5   L.R.O., QSP 54/9 (1651)
6   L.R.O., QSP 1094/13 (1716)
7   L.R.O. PR872, *Op. cit.*
8   *Preston Pilot*, 7 July 1838
9   *Ibid.*, 8 September 1838
10 *Ibid.*, 29 September 1838
11 *Ibid.*, 22 July 1854
12 *Preston Herald*, 26 March 1881
13 L.R.O., UD/Lo 1/4

Chapter 5: Military History

1   L.R.O., QSP 22/12 (1649)
2   L.R.O., QSB 1/295/37 (1647)
3   L.R.O., QSP 22/18 (1649)
4   L.R.O., QSP 26/17 (1649)
5   T. Smith, *History of Longridge*, p. 24
6   *Ibid.*, p. 99
7   L.R.O., QSP 218/19 (1661-62)
8   L.R.O., QSP 1178/12 (1721)
9   T. Smith, *History of Longridge*, p. 31
10 L.R.O., The Alston Book, PR872
11 *Preston Pilot*, 13 October 1855
12 *Ibid.*, 10 November 1855
13 *Ibid.*, 3 November 1855
14 L.R.O., QSP 685/10 (1690)

Chapter 6: Quarries and Reservoirs

1   T. Smith, *History of Longridge*, p. 44
2   *Preston Pilot*, 29 September 1838
3   *Ibid.*, 16 March 1850
4   *Ibid.*, 8 March 1856
5   *Ibid.*, 30 May 1857
6   T. Smith, *History of Longridge*,
    pp. 100–102)
7   *Preston Pilot*, 10 October 1840
8   Following information from
    Oakes, Preston: *Water Supplies
    through Three Centuries*
9   H. Bowtell, *Lesser Railways of
    Bowland Forest and Craven
    Country* (1988)
10 *Ibid.*

*Chapter 7: Cottages and Cottage
Industries*

1   L.R.O., DDH 994 and DDH 996
2   L.R.O., DDH 1001 and DDH 1004
3   Private Deeds
4   T. Smith, *History of Longridge*,
    pp. 110,111
5   P.R.O., National Census 1851
6   E. Hopwood, *A History of the
    Lancashire Cotton Industry & the
    Amalgamated Weavers Association*
7   L.R.O., A List of Lancashire Wills
    proved within the Archdeaconry
    of Richmond – The Record
    Society, 1884
8   *Preston Pilot*, 28 August 1852
9   L.R.O., Tithe Schedule and Map
    for Alston, 1837.
10 Private Deeds

11 M. Rothwell, *Industrial Heritage
    of the Ribble Valley*, (1990) p. 68
12 T. Smith, *History of Longridge*,
    pp. 102-105
13 *Preston Pilot*, 17 September 1831
14 T. Smith, *Op. cit.*, p. 103
15 T. Smith, *Op. cit.*, p. 41
16 *Preston Pilot*, 6 June 1846
17 *Ibid.*, 30 October 1847
18 G. H. Wood, *History of Wages in
    the Cotton Trade*

Chapter 8: Newtown and its People

1   T. Smith, *History of Longridge*, p. 30
2   *Ibid.*, p. 30
3   L.R.O., Will & Inventory of Seth
    Eccles of Alston, 1724
4   T. Smith, *op. cit.*, p. 40
5   Information from Mrs E.
    Hardman, great grand daughter of
    the first Dr Eccles
6   Information from Matthew Brown
    & Co., Lion Brewery, Blackburn
7   *Ibid.*
8   *Preston Pilot*, 23 June 1832
9   *Ibid.*, 2 June 1827

Chapter 9: The Railway

1   N. Parker, *The Preston &
    Longridge Railway*, p. 4
2   *Preston Pilot*, 21 April 1838
3   *Ibid.*, 4 May 1839
4   *Ibid.*, 18 April 1840
5   *Ibid.*, 25 April 1840
6   *Ibid.*, 25 April 1840
7   *Ibid.*, 2 May 1840
8   *Ibid.*, 13 June 1840
9   *Ibid.*, 29 May 1841
10 *Ibid.*, 5 August 1843
11 *Ibid.*, 26 October 1844
12 *Ibid.*, 24 May 1845
13 *Ibid.*, 16 May 1846
14 *Ibid.*, 24 January 1846
15 *Ibid.*, 10 June 1848
16 *Ibid.*, 17 June 1848
17 C. Snow, *A Preston Railway
    Album*, p. 43
18 *Ibid.*, p. 45
19 N. Parker, *Op. cit.*, p. 12
20 *Preston Pilot*, 17 August 1867
21 *Ibid.*, 25 January 1868
22 *Ibid.*, 31 December 1859
23 *Ibid.*, 7 March 1868

24 *Ibid.*, 4 Septmeber 1858
25 *Ibid.*, 11 June 1859
26 N. Parker, *Op. cit.*, p. 22
27 N. Parker, *Op. cit.*, p. 22

Chapter 10: Mills and Factories

1   M. Rothwell, *Industrial Heritage of the Ribble Valley*, p. 66
2   P.R.O., National Census, 1841
3   M. Rothwell, *op. cit.*, pp. 66,67
4   M. Rothwell, *op. cit.*, p. 67
5   M. Rothwell, *op. cit.*, pp. 68,69
6   T. Smith, *History of Longridge*, p. 272
7   *Preston Pilot*, 22 October 1856
8   *Preston Pilot*, 21 April 1838
9   P.R.O., National Census, 1851
10 T. Smith, *History of Longridge*, p. 105
11 *Preston Pilot*, 31 May 1851
12 Census, 1861, *op. cit.*
13 *Preston Chronicle*, 3 April 1852
14 *Preston Pilot*, 20 August 1853
15 T. Smith, *op. cit.*, p. 46

Chapter 11: The Village Grows

1   *Preston Pilot*, 7 March 1868
2   T. Smith, *History of Longridge*, p. 88
3   *Ibid.*, pp. 88,89
4   *Ibid.*, p. 88
5   *Ibid.*, p. 88

Chapter 12: Inns & Beerhouses

1   *Preston Pilot*, 1 June 1844
2   *Ibid.*, 17 August 1844
3   Private Deeds
4   Referred to in *Preston Pilot* as Station Hotel in 1847, and as Towneley Arms in 1853.
5   *Preston Pilot*, 11 March 1848
6   *Ibid.*, 23 October 1847
7   *Ibid.*, 9 May 1846

Chapter 13: Meeting Spiritual Needs

1   F. Blundell, *Old Catholic Lancashire*, p. 173
2   *Ibid.*, p. 174
3   C. A. Bolton, *Salford Diocese and its Catholic Past*
4   *Ibid.*
5   Longridge Congregational Church Centenary Booklet, (1965)
6   *Ibid.*
7   *Ibid.*
8   *Ibid.*
9   A. Hewitson, *Our Country Churches and Chapels*, p. 102
10 *Ibid.*, p. 103
11 Longridge Methodist Church Centenary Booklet (1984)
12 Hewitson, *op. cit.*, p. 97
13 T. Smith, *History of Longridge*, p. 53
14 *Ibid.*, p. 58
15 Hewitson, *op. cit.*, p. 98
16 *Preston Pilot*, 7 August 1841
17 Hewitson, *op. cit.*, p. 96
18 Hewitson, *op. cit.*, p. 97
19 Smith, *Op. cit.*, p. 58
20 L.R.O., Longridge New Church, (1876)
21 *Ibid.*, p. 57
22 *Preston Herald*, 15 January 1881

Chapter 14: Alston College

1   T. Smith, *History of Longridge*, p. 217
2   *Preston Pilot*, 1 May 1858
3   L.R.O., Mortgage Indentures
4   North West Water Authority – Plans & Mortgages
5   *Preston Pilot*, 10 July 1858
6   L.R.O., Mortgage Indentures
7   Oakes, Preston: *Water Supplies through Three Centuries*
8   Smith, *op. cit.*, pp. 216,217

Chapter 15: Public Services

1   *Preston Pilot*, 14 February 1852
2   *Ibid.*, 3 November 1849
3   *Ibid.*, 10 November 1849
4   *Ibid.*, 17 November 1849
5   *Ibid.*, 30 March 1850
6   *Ibid.*, 25 May 1850
7   *Ibid.*, 20 October 1855
8   *Ibid.*, 8 February 1845
9   *Preston Pilot*, 23 December 1848
10 *Preston Pilot*, 26 October 1867
11 *Ibid.*, 21 December 1867
12 *Preston Herald*, 16 February 1881
13 *Ibid.*, 13 September 1890
14 *Ibid.*, 30 September 1905

Bibliography

Primary Sources

Public Record Office
National Census Returns

Lancashire Record Office
Probate Inventories
Quarter Sessions Petitions
The Alston Book
Transcriptions of the Ribchester Parish Register

Harris Library and Museum, Preston
Preston Pilot
Preston Chronicle
Preston Herald

North West Water Authority
Alston College Documents

Secondary Sources

Bagley, J. J. and Lewis, A. S., *Lancashire at War*, 1977
Blundell, Dom. F., *Old Catholic Lancashire*
Bolton, Charles A., *Salford Diocese and its Catholic Past*
Bowtell, Harold, *Lesser Railways of Bowland Forest and Craven Country*, 1988
Hewitson, *Our Country Churches and Chapels*
Hopwood, Edwin, *A History of the Lancashire Cotton Industry & the Amalgamated Weavers Association*
Longridge Congregational Church Centenary Booklet
Longridge Methodist Church Centenary Booklet

Oakes, *Water Supplies Through Three Centuries*

Parker, Norman, *The Preston & Longridge Railway*, 1972

Rothwell, Mike, *Industrial Heritage of the Ribble Valley*, 1990

Smith, T, *History of Longridge*, 1888

Snow, Chris, *A Preston Railway Album*

Stratton, J. M., *Agricultural Records*, 1978

Till, J. M. and M. R., *History of St. Lawrence with St. Paul, Longridge*, 1990

Wood, G. H., *History of Wages in the Cotton Trade.*

Index

List of Subscribers

J. B. and W. M. Aherne, Longridge
J. and E. Ainsworth, Longridge
Mrs Kate Akroyd, Ribchester
Bruce and Christine Alder, Longridge
Mr R. J. Allen, Longridge
Mrs A. M. Allibone, Longridge
Alston Lane R. C. Primary School,
    Longridge
David J. Altham, Longridge
Mr Neil Arrowsmith, Longridge
John Ashton, Longridge
Mrs D. E. Ashworth, Longridge
H. J. Atkinson, Longridge
Mr Hubert Baines, Longridge
Mrs D. Bamber, Longridge
Maureen Lynn Bamber, Longridge
Shirley Anne Bamber, Longridge
Mr and Mrs E. C. Barnes, Longridge
Steven and Helen Barsby, Longridge
Ron Bass, Longridge
Mr and Mrs G. R. Bevan, Longridge
Mr and Mrs R. J. Birch, Grimsargh
Mrs B. J. Blackburn, Longridge
J. Blackwell, Longridge
Mrs J. M. Booth, Ashton, Preston
Mr S. D. Bowes, Longridge
Mrs J. L. Bowker, Grimsargh
Paul Bowker, Longridge
Mrs P. Bradford, Longridge
Mr M. R. Brewer, Ribchester
Mr and Mrs K. Bridge, Longridge
Mr J. Bristo, Longridge
Mr William Bristo, Longridge
Mrs E. Brown, Longridge
Mrs F. Brown, Longridge
George Brown, Longridge
Marguerite Brown, Longridge
Mrs M. P. Brown, Chipping
Mrs Ivy Burch, Longridge
John Buxton, Longridge
Nellie Carbis, Grimsargh
Walter Carefoot, Longridge
J. K. Carter, Longridge
V. J. Carter, Chorley
Mr and Mrs F. A. Childs, Bamber Bridge
Chipping Local History Society
Miss D. F. Clay, Longridge
Walter Clayton, Longridge

Mr M. A. Clegg, Longridge
P. Clements, Longridge
Mr and Mrs S. W. Codling, Longridge
D. Collis, Longridge
Mrs Mary Cottam, Longridge
Margaret Lois Cowell, Longridge
Mr A. N. Craven, Longridge
Melvyn Croasdale, Longridge
Mrs Hilary E. Croft, Longridge
Mrs Ruby Croft, Grimsargh
E. Crompton, Anglesey
J. D. Cross, Longridge
M. and J. Crossthwaite, Longridge
Mrs Ena Davies, Longridge
Mrs Greta Davis, Longridge
Chris Dewhurst (Builders), Longridge
Mr J. P. Dodd, Longridge
Adam Thomas Dugdale, Longridge
L. Eastham, Whittingham
Mr and Mrs P. Eastham, Longridge
W. R. Eastham, Longridge
Mr G. Eccles, Longridge
Mrs Jacqueline Eccles, Longridge
James Eccles, Longridge
R. S. Edelston, Longridge
David Edmondson, Longridge
Denis Edmondson, Longridge
Mrs E. Edmondson, Longridge
James Edmondson, Longridge
Nigel Evans MP, Longridge
Mr John Fadden, Longridge
Mrs Joanne Fawcett, Longridge
Mrs Elizabeth Ffelan, Longridge
Mr and Mrs E. Finch, Longridge
Mr Andrew Paul Fordham
Mr David Anthony Fordham
Mr Ian Thomas Fordham
K. M. and J. M. Freeman, Longridge
Friends of St Mary's R.C. School, Chipping
Mrs Margaret Fryer, Longridge
Arthur Gibson, Longridge
Mr Mark Goodsell, Surrey
Mr A. R. Gornall, Longridge
Mr G Gornall, Longridge
Mr K. W. Gornall, Longridge
Robert Gornall, Longridge
Michael H. Gorton, Longridge
Mrs Winifred Grayston, Longridge

Mr and Mrs H. V. Greer, Co.Down
Mr I. Grimshaw, Longridge
D. and C. R. Gunnell, Longridge
I. J. Haley, Longridge
Mr J. Halsall, Longridge
Keith and Karen Hankinson, Longridge
Mr K. Hardman, Longridge
E. L. Harrison, Longridge
Mrs D. J. Haworth, Preston
Terry and Cheryl Haynes, Longridge
Mrs Elizabeth Heigh, Longridge
Robert James Hempton, Longridge
P. and J. Henshaw, Longridge
The Hill R.C. School, Goosnargh
Mrs C. Hodge, Cambridge
Mrs. C. M. Hodkinson, Longridge
Mrs Doreen Hoggarth, Grimsargh
Miss G. Holden, Longridge
John Holden, Longridge
Mr R. N. Hollinghurst, Longridge
Mr and Mrs John Holmes, Ribchester
Arnold and Hilary Hough, Longridge
Mr W. Houghton, Longridge
Peter and Elaine Howarth, Longridge
F. E. Hoyle, Chipping
David L. Humphreys, Longridge
Mr B. W. Hunt, Whittingham
R. T. Hunt, Longridge
Olive Hurlstone, Longridge
Mr and Mrs A. J. Hutcheson, Longridge
Mrs A. J. Hutchinson, Longridge
L. E. Ingham, Longridge
Mrs and Mrs J. A. Ireland, Longridge
Wilfred Ireland, Longridge
Mr T. A. Jackson, Longridge
Mrs E. Jennings, Longridge
Mr Keith Johnson, Longridge
Mr and Mrs W. R. Kay, Longridge
Mrs C. M. Kerfoot, Goosnargh
Raymond Leech, Longridge
Mr F. and Mrs D. Little, Longridge
Longridge C. P. School
Longridge High School
Longridge Sport and Leisure
Arthur and Mildred Lord, Shifnal
M. D. Lovat, Longridge
Barbara Lucas, Bolton
Mrs P. MacDonald, Longridge
Daniel McComb, Longridge
Diane McDonald, Longridge
Mrs R. McNamara, Grimsargh
Mrs Margaret Marsh, Longridge
Mr Thomas Henry Marsland, Chorley
A. K. Mason, Garstang
Jean Mayhew, Longridge

Mr Andrew Melling, Longridge
Arthur Mercer, Garstang
Michael Monks, Longridge
B. S. Muncaster, Woodplumpton
Nichols, Craven and Marsdens, Longridge
Mr Joe Nicholson, Longridge
Mrs Anne Nickolaus, Longridge
Mr Christopher Nolan, Longridge
Mr and Mrs D. Norman, Longridge
Miss M. J. Ogden, Longridge
Mr I. N. Page, West Yorks
D. Parker, London
M. and E. M. Parker, Grimsargh
Mr Brian Parkinson, Longridge
Mrs D. Parkinson, Longridge
Mrs I. Parkinson, Longridge
T. M. and P. M. Pattinson, Grimsargh
Mr and Mrs K. and J. Pickard, Longridge
T. P. and B. P. Piercy, Longridge
T. S. Pinder, Longridge
Mrs B. M. Piner, Longridge
Mr and Mrs G. V. Pollitt, Longridge
G. Porter, Longridge
Mr and Mrs F. Priest, Longridge
Mrs M. L. Procter, Longridge
N. J. Procter, Longridge
J. B. Ravenscroft, Longridge
J. S. Reese and A. J. Reese, Longridge
A. Rhodes, Longridge
Mr Brian Rhodes, Longridge
Mrs P. Rigby, Longridge
Roy C. Rigby, Longridge
Margaret Roberts, Longridge
Mr and Mrs J. V. Robinson, Longridge
Mrs Charmaine Rogers, Longridge
Mr B. Rowland, Whittingham
Mr and Mrs K. M. Sanderson, Longridge
Mrs Jean Seed, Longridge
Mr W. L. Seed, Clwyd
Mrs E. Simpson, Longridge
Miss J. M. Simpson, Longridge
Ann Isabelle Singleton, Longridge
D. Skilbeck, Longridge
Mr Maurice Skilbeck, Longridge
Mrs Alice Slater, Longridge
James Slater, Longridge
Mr M. B. Slater, Longridge
Ella Slinger, Bolton
Mrs Alan Smith, Sherbourne
Mr and Mrs D. Smith, Longridge
Eric Smith, Longridge
John D. Smith, Berwickshire
John Robert Smith, Longridge
Margaret E. Smith, Blackpool
Philip N. Smith, Longridge

Sheila Smith, Longridge
Mr William Smith, Longridge
Mr and Mrs Robert Sutton, Longridge
Arnold Swift and Son Ltd, Longridge
Mrs Doreen Taylor, Longridge
Mr H. and Mrs E. Till, Barton
John and Diane Till, Longridge
Sylvia and Peter Thomas, Longridge
A. Timbrell, Longridge
K. Tyrer, Longridge
Mrs A. Walker, Longridge
Miss H. Walker, Fulwood
Mr and Mrs J. Walker, Longridge
Raymond M. Walker, Longridge
Miss Lesley Ann Walmsley, Longridge
Richard Walmsley, Longridge
W. J. Walmsley, Longridge
Mr Richard Walne, Chipping
J. W. Walsh, Cheshire
Mr and Mrs B. S. Walton, Longridge
Mrs E. M. Wareing, Longridge
Mr Andrew Waring, Longridge
Joseph William Waring, Longridge

Mr D. E. Waters, Barton
Mr and Mrs Wearden, Longridge
Susan Welton, Longridge
Miss Brenda M. White, Longridge
Mr and Mrs T. White, Canada
William R. Whitaker, Longridge
Mrs J. Whittaker, Broughton
Group Captain Joseph G. Whitaker, Wokingham
William R. Whitaker, Longridge
Mr Gary and Patricia F. Wignall, Longridge
H. A. and T. M. Wilcock, Longridge
St Wilfrid's Primary School, Longridge
Gerald Wilkinson, Longridge
Miss M. A. Wilkinson, Longridge
Mr John Gordon Willan, Longridge
Mr Reginald Willan, Longridge
Mrs P. Williams, Longridge
Sheila Woan, Longridge
Sheila Woodburn, Longridge
Mrs D. M. Woods, Longridge
Mr C. G. Wooler, Longridge
Mr W. Young, Longridge